ROBINSON JEFFERS
Poet and Prophet

ROBINSON JEFFERS

Poet and Prophet

JAMES KARMAN

STANFORD UNIVERSITY PRESS

Stanford, California

Stanford University Press
Stanford, California

Printed on acid-free, archival-quality paper
Printed and bound in Great Britain by
Marston Book Services Ltd, Oxfordshire

Library of Congress Cataloging-in-Publication Data

Karman, James, author.
  Robinson Jeffers : poet and prophet / James Karman.
     pages cm
  Includes bibliographical references and index.
  ISBN 978-0-8047-8963-9 (pbk. : alk. paper)
  1. Jeffers, Robinson, 1887-1962. 2. Poets, American--20th century--Biography.
I. Title.
  PS3519.E27Z639 2015
  811'.52--dc23
  [B]
                                    2015008138

ISBN 978-0-8047-9550-0 (electronic)

Adapted from the design by Adrian Wilson for *The Collected Poetry of Robinson Jeffers*
Typeset by Bruce Lundquist in 12/15 Centaur MT

For
Paula Karman

CONTENTS

ILLUSTRATIONS

ROBINSON JEFFERS
Poet and Prophet

1 Big Sur, California, 1935

INTRODUCTION

> Very like leaves
> upon this earth are the generations of men—
> old leaves, cast on the ground by wind, young leaves
> the greening forest bears when spring comes in.
> So mortals pass; one generation flowers
> even as another dies away.
>
> Homer, *The Iliad*, Book VI

Robinson Jeffers was born January 10, 1887 and died January 20, 1962. He and his generation came of age at the beginning of the last century, during a time of extraordinary change. Among American-born poets, Jeffers, Ezra Pound, H. D. (Hilda Doolittle), Marianne Moore, and T. S. Eliot were all about the same age. Amy Lowell, Robert Frost, Carl Sandburg, Wallace Stevens, William Carlos Williams, and Sara Teasdale were a few years older; Edna St. Vincent Millay, Archibald MacLeish, and E. E. Cummings were a few years younger. Each was born with an artistic gift that, like a sail, caught the wind of human longing and cast them forth, in search of a creative and meaningful life.

The generation of poets that passed away around the time Jeffers and his contemporaries were born included Emily Dickinson, who died in 1886, and Walt Whitman, who died in 1892. As precursors, both showed those who followed how to find and use a personal voice, how to express deep truths in simple language, how to share both joy and pain with perfect candor.

Each of these lessons served Jeffers and his contemporaries well. As they looked back at the nineteenth century, the Western tradition, and all of human history behind them, and as they looked forward to the twentieth century and the unknown human future stretching out before, they were emboldened to start fresh, to "make it new," as Pound said, and to meet the world on their own terms. In them and through them, Modern poetry was born.

As time progressed and the twentieth century ran its course, critical regard for each poet fluctuated. Jeffers became famous, virtually overnight, with the publication of *Tamar and Other Poems* in 1924 and the expanded *Roan Stallion, Tamar and Other Poems* in 1925. By the end of the decade, with three additional books of candescent verse on bookstore shelves, he was arguably the most famous poet in America. When two more books soon followed, *Time* magazine took note and featured a portrait photograph of Jeffers, taken by his friend Edward Weston, on the cover of the April 4, 1932 issue. Jeffers remained popular through the 1930s, but by the end of the decade a number of influential critics had turned against him. In the 1940s, despite the overwhelming international success of his play *Medea*, written for and performed on Broadway by Judith Anderson, Jeffers' reputation continued to slide. His poetry won honors in the 1950s, and his plays were performed around the world, yet many critics dismissed him—prompting Horace Gregory to ask, in a 1954 *New York Herald Tribune* essay titled "The Disillusioned Wordsworth of Our Age,"

"'Why does so much deep silence surround the name of Robinson Jeffers?'" This is a question that has puzzled attentive readers ever since.

In some ways, the question is misleading, for Jeffers has always had a wide audience. Tor House, his home in Carmel, California, is now a National Historic Landmark, visited by several thousand people every year; the Robinson Jeffers Association, an organization of scholars, publishes *Jeffers Studies* and hosts an annual conference devoted to his work; and books and articles about Jeffers continue to assess his achievement. Recent additions to an expanding list of publications include *Robinson Jeffers and the American Sublime* by Robert Zaller and *Inventing the Language to Tell It: Robinson Jeffers and the Biology of Consciousness* by George Hart. Forthcoming books include *The Wild That Attracts Us: New Critical Essays on Robinson Jeffers* edited by ShaunAnne Tangney, *Towers of Myth and Stone: Yeats's Influence on Robinson Jeffers* by Deborah Fleming, and a comprehensive descriptive bibliography by Michael Broomfield.

In other ways, the silence surrounding Jeffers is easy to understand. As an anti-modern Modernist, his poetry is fundamentally different in both form and content from that of his contemporaries, and critics have devoted most of their attention to mainstream verse.

A typical modern poem, for instance, is composed in the lyric mode—a short form concerned primarily with the expression of subjective thoughts, perceptions, and experiences. While there are many exceptions, the setting of a modern poem is usually current in time and place, diction leans toward the colloquial, lines are short, rhythms free, and a variety of devices (such as ambiguity, discontinuity, and irony) are used to complicate meaning.

Jeffers also composed lyric poems, but he devoted equal attention to narrative verse and drama. These long poetic forms, all but abandoned by others, provided Jeffers with opportunities for impersonal observation, the depiction of life in different historical settings, character development, and dialogue. His lines were usually long, sometimes extending to twenty words or more, and employed complex, organic rhythms based on heartbeats, tidal recurrences, and other natural measures. In an effort to avoid obscurity, he used poetic devices to stabilize and clarify meaning.

With regard to content, the difference between Jeffers and his contemporaries was even greater. Jeffers was the only major poet of his time who lived in the far west, and much of his poetry attempts to capture the beauty of the wild Pacific shore. People were important to him—indeed, a main theme of his work involves their tragic suffering—but he saw human history within the context of natural history, and, with an evolutionary view of life in mind, he embraced an astronomical and geological view of time. From that vantage point, all existence, including that of the entire human species, was ephemeral. As he surveyed the course of history—writing of Greece, Rome, the birth of Christendom, the Middle Ages, modern Europe, and America—he saw each cultural moment, and civilization as a whole, as wave-like, destined to rise, fall, and ultimately dissolve away.

Jeffers' experience of deep time added a vatic amplitude to his verse, and a sharp moral edge. He spoke repeatedly about the destruction of Earth's environment, warning, shrilly at times, of the effects of overpopulation, pollution, and the exploitation of natural resources. He also studied the mystery of human cruelty, and condemned violence on all levels: against animals, between persons, within families, and amongst nations. Jeffers was particularly concerned with the manifestation of cruelty in love—or, more narrowly, from a Darwinian and Freudian perspective, in sex—and he examined the destructive complications of desire with a frankness that appalled some readers. The cruelty of war was another major theme of his work, and his reflections on the two main conflagrations of his time, World War I and World War II, were among the most bitter and searing of the century.

In Jeffers' denunciation of war, and in his excoriation of world leaders (Roosevelt included), some readers heard the furious voice of a biblical prophet, and, given his upbringing, that voice may in fact be there. Jeffers rejected the biblical tradition, however, along with Christianity, all organized religions, and spiritual leaders in general. Nevertheless, his poetry is permeated with philosophical and religious concerns, and much of it is devoted to the search for Truth, Beauty, and the Good—a fool's errand, in the eyes of many. Jeffers found all three in a pantheistic view of nature and, thus, in a direct experience of God.

When Jeffers died in 1962, his friend Mark Van Doren wrote a eulogy that was published in the *Proceedings* of the American Academy of Arts and Letters. People thought of Jeffers, he says, as a remote and solitary figure—"a man of improbable, grim, abstracted beauty, indeed a hawk, a figure of granite, rather than a man at all"—but, to those who knew him, he "was affectionate and humorous, warm-hearted and courtly." Some people, he adds, regarded Jeffers' poetry as "uncompromising" and, because of the way it challenges accepted norms, "unacceptable." But one need not agree with Jeffers, Van Doren says, to appreciate him: "If Jeffers was wrong he will be wrong forever, and he would be the first to admit this. Right or wrong, however, his poems have power. And this power, at a guess, will last into other centuries than this one which he thought so pitifully mistaken."

Was Jeffers wrong? Decades before anyone worried about the effects of unbridled development on the environment, or disasters like Love Canal and the *Exxon Valdez* oil spill, Jeffers mourned "the broken balance, the hopeless prostration of the earth / Under men's hands and their minds, / The beautiful places killed like rabbits to make a city, / The spreading fungus, the slime-threads / And spores; my own coast's obscene future" ("The Broken Balance"). Long before anyone raised concerns about the shootings at Kent State, the beatings in Selma, Alabama, or the transformation of the United States into a militarized superpower, Jeffers said "beware . . . of the police in armed imperial America" ("I Shall Laugh Purely"). And years before *jihad* became a familiar word all around the world, Jeffers saw a looming threat: "Faith returns, beautiful, terrible, ridiculous, / And men are willing to die and kill for their faith. / Soon come the wars of religion; centuries have passed / Since the air so trembled with intense faith and hatred" ("Thebaid").

Right or wrong, the issues raised by Jeffers remain pressing; they are at the very center of public life; and the way we address them in coming years will affect, as Jeffers knew, not only the future of America, but the fate of humanity. The time is propitious, it seems, for a reexamination of Jeffers and for a careful consideration of the insights his poetry contains.

Jeffers' artistic vision is recorded in his work: eighteen volumes of verse published in the course of a fifty-year career. The entire achievement is contained in *The Collected Poetry of Robinson Jeffers*, edited by Tim Hunt and published in five volumes by Stanford University Press. Details of Jeffers' life are recorded in *The Collected Letters of Robinson Jeffers, with Selected Letters of Una Jeffers*, published in three volumes by Stanford University Press. Together, the *Collected Poetry* and the *Collected Letters* document Jeffers' distinguished contribution to America's literary and cultural history.

The concise biography that follows is a revised version of my introduction to volume one of the *Collected Letters*, where it served as an overview of Jeffers' life and work—one that could be read as a continuous narrative, or, for readers seeking a deeper understanding of moments in time when specific letters were written, as a series of chronological episodes. The purpose of the introduction was to identify the people, issues, and events that shaped Jeffers, to list and describe each of his major books, and to explain his response to and place in the modern world. That purpose remains the same in this edition. Readers who desire more than an overview, or who are curious about particular details mentioned in the text, should turn to the *Collected Letters*, where the full arc of Jeffers' life is traced through correspondence, and where he and Una tell their story in their own words. Key portions of that story—such as family life at Tor House, travels, marital conflicts, and relationships with friends—can only be understood through a study of the letters, together with the explanatory notes that accompany them.

Complete texts of the poems and essays by Jeffers cited in this biography can be found in either the *Collected Poetry* or the *Collected Letters* (with the exception of *The Alpine Christ*, which is only available in *The Alpine Christ and Other Poems*, edited by William Everson). Many of the poems are also included in *The Selected Poetry of Robinson Jeffers*, edited by Tim Hunt, and in *The Wild God of the World: An Anthology of Robinson Jeffers*, edited by Albert Gelpi.

For most citations, basic source information is provided within the text. In many instances, additional documentation can be found in the *Collected Letters*. Historical facts—such as population statistics and wartime casualty figures—are drawn from widely available public sources and government documents.

I. WILD HONEY

But now, as I smelled the wild honey midway the trestle and meditated the direction of modern poetry, my discouragement blackened. It seemed to me that Mallarmé and his followers, renouncing intelligibility in order to concentrate the music of poetry, had turned off the road into a narrowing lane. Their successors could only make further renunciations; ideas had gone, now meter had gone, imagery would have to go; then recognizable emotions would have to go; perhaps at last even words might have to go or give up their meaning, nothing be left but musical syllables. Every advance required the elimination of some aspect of reality, and what could it profit me to know the direction of modern poetry if I did not like the direction? It was too much like putting out your eyes to cultivate the sense of hearing, or cutting off the right hand to develop the left. These austerities were not for me. . . .

Circa 1914—from the introduction to
Roan Stallion, Tamar and Other Poems

1887–1905

For one destined to become a visionary poet concerned with nature, civilization, and the fate of humankind, Jeffers could not have had a better nor a more intellectually challenging childhood. He was born in Allegheny, Pennsylvania, now a part of Pittsburgh, and raised in nearby Sewickley and Edgeworth. His father, Dr. William Hamilton Jeffers, was a Presbyterian minister and professor of church history, biblical literature, and ancient languages (Greek,

Latin, Hebrew, Aramaic, Syriac, Arabic, Babylonian, and Assyrian). At the time Robinson was born, Dr. Jeffers was forty-nine and teaching at Western Theological Seminary in Allegheny. Jeffers' mother, Annie Tuttle Jeffers, was twenty-seven.

Dr. Jeffers had been married once before. His first wife, Louisa Maria Robinson, was the daughter of Thomas and Margaret Robinson, a prosperous Ohio couple involved in farming and cattle dealing. The Robinsons' only other child, a son named Clark, died in infancy. Dr. Jeffers and Louisa married in 1868. In 1869 Louisa remained with her parents when her husband embarked upon a study tour of Egypt, the Middle East, and Greece. When Dr. Jeffers returned, the couple moved to Wooster, Ohio, where Dr. Jeffers accepted a position at the University of Wooster. Their son William "Willie" Robinson Jeffers was born in February 1872. He died of cholera the following July during a visit to the home of his maternal grandparents. The couple had no other children. Louisa died in 1882 as a result of "paralysis." How long she had been disabled prior to her death is unknown. Louisa's mother died the year before while visiting the Jeffers home, and her father died the year after, broken by his losses. The entire family is buried at Green Lawn Cemetery in Columbus, Ohio. Dr. Jeffers placed a large memorial obelisk at the gravesite, with "Robinson" inscribed on one side and "Jeffers" on the other.

Dr. Jeffers met his second wife, Annie Tuttle, at the home of her foster parents, John and Philena Robinson (no known relation to Louisa's family), who lived in Sewickley. A brief engagement led to marriage in April 1885 and the birth of their first son, John Robinson Jeffers, in 1887. A second son, Hamilton Moore Jeffers, was born in 1893.

Jeffers' parents preferred his middle name (possibly given with Dr. Jeffers' first wife in mind), so he was always called Robinson or Robin. As a little boy he attended private schools in Pittsburgh and received additional lessons from his father at home. Instruction in Greek came first, along with study of the Bible and church doctrine, and then Latin. When Robinson was eleven, having already visited Europe six years before, he was enrolled in a school in Leipzig so he could study Greek and Latin while learning German. The following year he was sent to a school in Vevey, Switzerland in order to further his classical studies while learning French. Courses in Greek, Latin, and other basic subjects, taught in French or German, continued in Switzerland for three more years. Jeffers' mother, who spoke French and was an accomplished musician, stayed in Europe with her son at this time; Jeffers' father joined them each summer.

A September 1901 letter (located in the archives of the Pittsburgh Theological Seminary), written by Annie in Zurich to her husband in the United States, provides a glimpse into Robinson's academic regimen. Knowing that Dr. Jeffers regarded German as the language of scholars, especially in the field of philology, and anticipating his professorial concern, she tells him that Robinson "is translating his Latin into French still instead of German; his teacher is an Italian & does not know German well enough to translate into it." In regard to frequency of use, English was Jeffers'

2 Robinson Jeffers, 1899

third working language when he lived in Europe; it was his fifth language overall, counting Greek and Latin.

Dr. Jeffers brought his family back to America in 1902. At fifteen, Robinson enrolled as a sophomore at Western University of Pennsylvania, now called the University of Pittsburgh. For a curriculum he selected the Classical Course, which allowed him to continue along the path already laid out for him. According to the university catalog, the Classical Course was designed to help students become "well versed in ancient languages, German, French, and English Literature, with the usual courses in Science and Mathematics."

It is worth noting that the acting chancellor of the university at the time Robinson was there was John A. Brashear, one of Pittsburgh's most famous and popular citizens. Brashear was a self-taught mechanical genius who became a celebrated astronomer and manufacturer of precision scientific instruments. The telescopes he made were among the best in the world. As a director of the Allegheny Observatory and as a committed educator (who had a special interest in reaching out to children), Brashear helped make Pittsburgh a center for astronomical research. Jeffers' own lifelong interest in the stars may have been stimulated by the attention given astronomy in his hometown. The same could be said for his younger brother Hamilton, who eventually earned a Ph.D. in the field and devoted his career to research at Lick Observatory.

In 1903 Dr. Jeffers retired from teaching at the seminary and, wanting to live in a healthier climate, moved his family to southern California. Soon thereafter he purchased property and built a home in Highland Park, a suburb of Los Angeles. As an accomplished public speaker, Dr. Jeffers participated in chautauqua programs in Los Angeles and remained active in Presbyterian Church councils. Robinson was given advanced standing at Occidental College in Highland Park and, though younger than his fellow students, participated fully in college life. He joined and later became an officer of the Philomathian Society, a literary club, and served as literary editor of the *Occidental* (formerly known as the *Aurora*), the college newspaper. He published poems in the paper and also composed and recited them for official college events. By the time Jeffers graduated in 1905, at age eighteen, he had also published poems in the *Los Angeles Times* and in two national magazines, the *Youth's Companion* and *Out West*. His parents were no doubt anxious to see what their precocious son would do next.

1905—1910

"In or about December, 1910, human character changed." This famous assertion, which appears in a 1924 essay by Virginia Woolf titled "Mr. Bennett and Mrs. Brown" (also titled "Character in Fiction"), is often used to date the beginning of the Modern Age. Woolf makes the same point a little later in her essay when she says "All human relations have shifted—those between masters and servants, husbands and wives, parents and children. And when human relations change there is at the same time a change in religion, conduct, politics, and literature. Let us agree to place one of these changes about the year 1910." While Woolf is referring to the end of the Edwardian Age and the beginning of the Georgian Age in England, her observation has been applied to a seismic shift felt around the world. Novelists who lived at that time, she says, had to invent new ways to capture reality in words, especially the interior reality of their protagonists. The same challenge faced other writers. Old ways of doing things no longer worked: "And so the smashing and the crashing began. Thus it is that we hear all around us, in poems and novels and biographies, even in newspaper articles and essays, the sound of breaking and falling, crashing and destruction." What was true for writers was true for other artists. Indeed, among the intelligentsia in Europe and America, an unsettled feeling around 1910 was pandemic.

Jeffers himself was something of a lost soul at the time. After graduating from Occidental in the spring of 1905, he decided to pursue graduate studies at the University of Southern California in the fall. Along with courses in Spanish, Old English, and Oratory, Jeffers enrolled in Advanced German, which featured a reading of Goethe's *Faust*. He left the University of Southern California after the spring semester and traveled with his parents to Switzerland, where he entered the University of Zurich. His curriculum there included Introduction to Philosophy, Old English Literature, French Literature from 1840 to 1900, Dante's Life and Work, Spanish Romance Poetry, and History of the Roman Empire. Though others might have struggled with courses requiring facility with several languages at once—Old English, French, Italian, Spanish, and Latin, with lectures in French and German—Jeffers was right at home. Nevertheless, he abandoned his studies after a semester and returned to California alone.

Jeffers drifted for several more months, during which time he translated German medical papers for his mother's physician. Intrigued by the science involved, he enrolled in the Medical School at the University of Southern California in the fall of 1907. He also joined a fraternity, caroused with friends, wrote poetry, and competed in sports. In November he tried out for the cross-country team, earning a berth by finishing among the top six runners in a 4-mile race. The winner completed the distance in 24 minutes and 58 seconds, so Jeffers' pace was close to that. Following two years of preparatory work, Jeffers entered the College of Physicians and Surgeons, where he distinguished himself as the best student in his classes. After his third year of studies, however, he lost interest in medicine and decided to pursue a forestry degree at the University of Washington in Seattle. His mother and father accompanied him to Seattle, and he enrolled in courses there in the fall of 1910, but he did not complete them. A few months passed before he gave up and returned to Los Angeles, uncertain what to do.

Jeffers' goals for the future, his relationship to his parents, and his sense of himself were all called into question by another problem in 1910: he was deeply in love with a married woman named Una.

Una Lindsay (Call) Kuster was born in Mason, Michigan, January 6, 1884. At age seventeen, seeking adventure and a good education, she left her hometown and moved to Berkeley, where she enrolled at the University of California.

An older half-sister who lived in San Francisco acted as a guardian and chaperone. Una soon met Edward Gerhard Kuster, a young man who had graduated from Berkeley in 1900 and was completing his studies in law. Teddie, as he was called, was the son of a Los Angeles physician and a member of a wealthy extended family. He qualified for the California bar in 1902, married Una in May of that year, and began his career as a well-connected Los Angeles attorney. Kuster's success in the courtroom was soon matched by his increasing social stature. He was a member of several athletic and country clubs, he performed as a cellist with the Los Angeles Symphony, and he served as a leader of the newly formed Automobile Club of Southern California. Una joined him in some of his activities, but she was more interested in completing her education than in helping her husband advance his career. She entered the University of Southern California in the fall of 1905. One of her classes the following spring was Advanced German—the same class Jeffers was in.

The friendship between Robinson and Una, which began in 1906 with the study of *Faust*, continued through the following years. The two saw each other regularly on campus when Robinson was in medical school and Una was earning her degrees, a B.A. in 1908 and an M.A. in philosophy in 1910. Their friendship gradually deepened into love, and by the time Jeffers decided to study forestry in Seattle, their passion was all-consuming. In a letter dated September 14, 1910 (one of the few that survive from this time), written to Robinson when he was on his way north, Una expresses her longing and despair: "I didnt mean to cry today," she says,

"I meant to show you how brave I could be,—but not to see your dear eyes—not to feel your lips against my throat— — the intolerable pain I am to feel through endless months, came over me like a flood." A letter written the following day repeats the same lament:

I do not see how I am to live, very dearest,—I cannot see anything ahead for many months but unending blankness—How can I tell you my utter love—my utter devotion, but—you know it! I do not think that time or distance or evil circumstance—or—cruelty can separate us anymore. I am yours and I shall walk softly all my days until we can take each others hands and fare forth for those wild red vivid joys we two must know together.

Despite such love, or partly because of it, when Jeffers abandoned his plans in Seattle and returned to Los Angeles, his situation seemed hopeless. He was twenty-three, five years had passed since he finished his only degree, he was romantically involved with a married woman, and he had no vocational prospects. He began to drink heavily and spend his days in idleness.

If there is truth to Virginia Woolf's assertion that a seismic shift occurred in 1910 that disquieted artists and intellectuals around the world, then Jeffers' torment was doubtless more complicated. Indeed, for sensitive individuals like Jeffers, stress was felt along a variety of cultural, intellectual, and spiritual fault lines.

Jeffers had been raised during the Gilded Age in America—at the very peak of that period, the Gay Nineties. He grew up in Pittsburgh, the thriving city of Andrew Carnegie and Henry Clay Frick. Educated in Europe, he experienced all the pleasures of La Belle Époque, including a full measure of Swiss gentility. In the major capitals of Europe and America, he saw construction on a grand scale: new schools, libraries, museums, hospitals, government headquarters, opera houses, orchestra halls, and private mansions graced just-widened boulevards and looked out upon beautiful gardens and stately parks. Many of the buildings were designed in the popular Beaux-Arts style and thus recaptured an earlier Baroque splendor. When Jeffers moved to California, he fulfilled a dream shared by millions of people: a chance to live in the fabled land of health, wealth, and sunshine, where opportunities were endless and anything was possible. He also witnessed the invention of the automobile, the airplane, and other technological wonders that, at the cultural level, were changing the world.

Intellectually, however, he knew that many great thinkers of the recent past had grave doubts about Western Civilization, even human life as a whole. Despite the ebullience of La Belle Époque, a *fin de siècle* miasma filled the air. Artists affiliated with the Decadent movement, for instance, believed Western Civilization had reached a state of decay and was on the way to death. They questioned the gaudy materialism they saw around them; they were tired of ordinary pleasures, especially those provided by cities; and they sought relief from boredom through art, immorality, and exaggerated behavior. Their feelings of estrangement and disaffection were similar to those found in Bohemian circles and among a restless avant-garde.

Their feelings were also shared, in one form or another, by the great artists and intellectuals of the nineteenth and early twentieth centuries, most of whom were driven by a desire to confront people in power, to condemn injustice, to expose the emptiness of established institutions, to ridicule stupidity, to explore the torments of the human soul, to find new ways to live, or to simply tell the plain truth about the way things are. Their goal, as Emerson said in "Self-Reliance," expressing a sentiment many endorsed, was to "affront and reprimand the smooth mediocrity and squalid contentment of the times." That was Marx's intent, too—even more so, given his absolute disdain for bourgeois culture—and his critique of the Western tradition was, by Jeffers' time, gathering ever-greater force. Darwin's ideas had a similar effect, insofar as they undercut settled opinions concerning the origin and destiny of humankind. And suddenly Freud's theories, as expounded in *The Interpretation of Dreams* (1900), and other pathbreaking books, demanded consideration. Einstein published his "Special Theory of Relativity" in 1905, and Picasso painted *Les Demoiselles d'Avignon* in 1907. Wherever Jeffers turned he saw upheaval.

Spiritually, Jeffers was open-minded. Despite the rigorous religious training he received from his father, he never gave himself fully to the church, and his father seems to have been wise enough to leave his son alone. Jeffers' inclinations, in this regard, appear to have followed the course set by the majority of nineteenth-century thinkers—the course of skepticism, spiritual independence, and disdain for rituals and creeds. Within the American tradition, this course was laid out by such key thinkers as Emerson, Thoreau, Whitman, and Dickinson, each of whom turned their backs on the traditional church, repudiated the special authority of the Bible, rejected conventional beliefs concerning Jesus, questioned the existence of the Christian God, and sought, primarily in nature, direct contact with the sacred.

Walt Whitman, for example, wanted nothing less than total revolution. "Unscrew the locks from the doors!" he says, exalting freedom, "Unscrew the doors themselves from their jambs!" To live authentically, Whitman believed, people must be natural and unrestrained.

This requires, at the physical level of existence, a celebration of sense experience and the pleasures of the body. "I Sing the Body Electric," the title of one of Whitman's poems, expresses the raison d'être for his work as a whole. We see this in "Song of Myself," where Whitman describes his work as a poet in physical terms: "This is the press of a bashful hand, this the float and odor of hair, / This the touch of my lips to yours, this the murmur of yearning." Desire saturates *Leaves of Grass* (1891–1892), as does the satisfaction of desire: "I merely stir, press, feel with my fingers, and am happy, / To touch my person to some one else's is about as much as I can stand." With a candor that still seems bold, Whitman placed sexuality at the center of art and life. Denouncing prudery in a letter written to Emerson in 1856, Whitman extols openness:

To me, henceforth, that theory of any thing, no matter what, stagnates in its vitals, cowardly and rotten, while it cannot publicly accept, and publicly name, with specific words, the things on which all existence, all souls, all realization, all decency, all health, all that is worth being here for, all of woman and of man, all beauty, all purity, all sweetness, all friendship, all strength, all life, all immortality depend. The courageous soul . . . may be proved by faith in sex, and by disdaining concessions.

Not only should people talk about physical love, they should also freely express it. "For the one I love most lay sleeping by me under the same cover in the cool night," he writes, recalling a moment of deep contentment. "In the stillness in the autumn moonbeams his face was inclined toward me, / And his arm lay lightly around my breast—And that night I was happy."

Coincident with Whitman's concern for the body was his concern for the soul, which he believed should also be unconstrained. "What do you suppose will satisfy the soul, except to walk free and own no superior?" he wonders. Since there is no God in heaven demanding obedience and worship, "Why should I pray? why should I venerate and be ceremonious?" he asks. "The old cautious hucksters," such as Jehovah, Zeus, Allah, and other deities, are interesting as mythic archetypes, as "rough deific sketches," but, ultimately, they must be set aside. An awakened soul knows that God is in a blade of grass, a morning glory by the window, a wren's egg—not in the Bible, a church, or some judgment-seat above. "Why should I wish to see God better than this day?" Whitman asks. "I see something of God each hour of the twenty-four, and each moment then, / In the faces of men and women I see God, and in my own face in the glass." An unfettered soul knows life is an endless pilgrimage, "a perpetual journey" without a destination, where every moment of the here and now, blissful or agonized, is consecrated.

The latter, agony, is something Whitman knew all too well. As a hospital aid during the Civil War, he nursed countless soldiers, hearing their stories, dressing their wounds. He already knew, of course, that life is difficult, but the war deepened his understanding of pain, as did the assassination of President Lincoln. Life's journey, he realized, for an individual as well as for a country, is sometimes "A march in the ranks hard-prest, and the road unknown, / A route through a heavy wood with muffled steps in the darkness."

A similar insight marks the work of Emily Dickinson. In fact, of all the major American authors, she may have walked the furthest down the *via negativa*. Most people, afraid of that dark path, are unwilling to follow after. Many of her poems are buoyant and uplifting, but her work as a whole has an incredibly dense specific gravity. "For each ecstatic instant," she writes, "We must an anguish pay"—at a ratio heavily weighted on the side of suffering: "For each beloved hour / Sharp pittances of years— / Bitter contested farthings— / And Coffers heaped with Tears!" (Poem 125). A list of representative first lines indicates the direction of her thoughts: "I like a look of agony"; "After great pain, a formal feeling comes—"; "I measure every Grief I meet"; "There is a pain—so utter—"; "Pain—has an Element of Blank—"; "I lived on dread"; "The loneliness one dare not sound"; "I should not dare to be so sad." As she says, describing her own personality, "I can wade Grief— / Whole Pools of it— / I'm used to that— / But the least push of Joy / Breaks up my feet—" (Poem 252).

The pain Dickinson probes is familiar to all; it is concerned with longing, loss, heartbreak, death—the thousand natural shocks, as Hamlet says, that flesh is heir to. But the pain is also deeper, more central to the human condition, and thus, for those willing to confront it, more profound. It arises from a state of utter hopelessness, of the sort experienced by a person lost at sea without anything to cling to, without "even a Report of Land— / To justify—Despair" (Poem 510). If land is in sight, anguish has a reason and a reference; but if one is all alone in the middle of nowhere, buffeted by waves and about to die, surrounded by a silent, empty horizon (which, in her bleakest moments, is how Dickinson pictured human existence), then despair itself is stifled. Beyond fear and pity, beyond panic, anger, and blame, nothing is left, not even abjection.

One source for this feeling was Dickinson's experience of God. An independent thinker in all areas, including faith, she once said of her family, "They are religious—except me—and address an Eclipse, every morning—whom they call their 'Father.'" Sometimes, Dickinson seems to catch a glimpse of a living God behind the Eclipse; in these instances, her poems express a familiar piety. Most often, though, she writes about the Eclipse itself, the seemingly dead God of the Judeo-Christian tradition, and then her poems are boldly iconoclastic. "The Bible is an antique Volume— / Written by faded Men," she says in one poem; "Of Course—I prayed— / And did God Care?" she asks in another (Poems 1545 and 376). In former days, when faith was innocent and vital, people believed they knew where they would go when they died—that is, to "God's Right Hand." But, she says, reflecting on the disappearance of God in her own time, "That Hand is amputated now / And God cannot be found" (Poem 1551). People, bewildered by the emptiness they feel, go on worshipping anyway. They pretend everything is fine: "Faith slips—and laughs, and rallies— / Blushes, if any see— / Plucks at a twig of Evidence— / And asks a Vane, the way." In church, there is still "Much Gesture from the Pulpit" and, loud as ever, "Strong Hallelujahs roll." With no response from above, though, such palliatives are ineffective: "Narcotics cannot still the Tooth / That nibbles at the soul—" (Poem 501).

Dickinson sums up her experience of the pain of life in a small poem about grief. Having experienced two devastating losses, she wonders if a third event "So huge, so hopeless to conceive / As these that twice befell" might yet remain to crush her. Linking her own situation to humanity's greater anguish in a world without God, she says that "Parting"— solitude, isolation, abandonment—"Parting is all we know of heaven / And all we need of hell" (Poem 1732).

In European literature, it was left to Friedrich Nietzsche—whom Jeffers read—to forthrightly announce the Death of God. As Nietzsche tells the story in *The Gay Science*, a madman runs into a marketplace looking for the deity. Ridiculed by the people assembled there, the madman says *"We have killed him*—you and I." In trying to describe the enormity of the situation, the madman asks a series of questions—questions that, given the intensity of Jeffers' encounter with his time and the pressure of his own existential distress, no doubt echoed in his ears:

What did we do when we unchained this earth from its sun? Whither is it moving now? Away from all suns? Are we not perpetually falling? Backward, sideward, forward, in all directions? Is there any up or down left? Are we not straying as through an infinite nothing? Do we not feel the breath of empty space? Has it not become colder? Is more and more night not coming on all the time?

1910—1915

"It was in 1915 the old world ended," says D. H. Lawrence in *Kangaroo* (Chapter 12, "The Nightmare"). This observation, like Woolf's, has also been used to identify the moment in Western history when tradition fell apart and the Modern Age began. In seeking to comprehend that milestone, Lawrence focused on the death involved, particularly the death of one symbolic city. "In the winter 1915–1916 the spirit of the old London collapsed," he says; "the city, in some way, perished, perished from being a heart of the world, and became a vortex of broken passions, lusts, hopes, fears, and horrors." Others could say the same for Paris, Berlin, Vienna, and Moscow. Each was at the center of a storm that was demolishing Europe. By the end of 1915, the Great War had been raging for almost a year and a half. Archduke Francis

Ferdinand was long since dead. The *Lusitania* with its 1,200 innocents lay in wreckage at the bottom of the sea. Barbed wire barricades and muddy trenches filled with rats and soldiers riddled the landscape. Heavy artillery and machine guns were backed by a new weapon of mass destruction: poison gas. In Ypres, after the second battle there, in what otherwise might have been a beautiful spring, 100,000 soldiers were dead, wounded, or missing. In Gallipoli in December, the toll was 400,000. And the storm had just begun.

Seeking to escape constant reminders of destruction, the protagonists of Lawrence's semi-autobiographical novel decide to leave London. "It was in mid-winter, 1915," he says, "that Somers and Harriet went down to Cornwall. The spirit of the war—the spirit of collapse and of human ignominy, had not travelled so far yet. It came in advancing waves."

The spirit of collapse had not yet hit America either. Americans were mindful of events on the other side of the Atlantic at the close of 1915, and they responded with sympathy or outrage to all that was happening there, but they were not yet aware of the magnitude of the conflict nor of the role they would soon play.

Much had happened in Jeffers' life by this time. His ongoing relationship with Una was discovered by her husband early in 1912. Teddie was shattered by the revelation. The fact of Una's sexual infidelity was difficult enough for him to deal with, but when he learned that Robinson made love to Una under the roof he had provided, it was more than he could endure. He and Una agreed that it would be best for them to separate for a while and that it would be wise for her to

3 Robinson Jeffers, ca. 1911

4 Una Call Kuster, 1911

avoid contact with Robinson, so in April 1912 Una left Los Angeles for an extended trip to Europe. She stayed through October, spending most of her time in England, Scotland, and Ireland, but also journeying to Germany, Austria, Italy, Switzerland, and France. While she was away, Una nurtured a hope that her marriage could be saved. With deep regret, Teddie realized this would be impossible. In July, believing it would be best for both of them, he initiated divorce proceedings. Soon after, he began to court Edith Emmons, the young woman who would become his second wife. By the time Una returned to America, her marriage to Teddie was behind her. She was free to resume her relationship with Robinson—which she did—and found in him and in herself a wellspring of undiminished passion.

When Una was in Europe, Robinson decided to return to the University of Washington and try again to study forestry. In January 1913, following a two-month stay in Berkeley, Una joined him in Seattle. Robinson and Una were married August 2, 1913, the day after her divorce was granted. Soon after, Una discovered she was pregnant. This knowledge, along with Robinson's realization that he was not suited to forestry (especially the business side of the profession), persuaded them to leave Seattle and return to Los Angeles where they could be near friends and Robinson's parents until the baby arrived. Their child, Maeve, was born May 5, 1914, but she only lived one day. In their sadness, they began making plans for a new life in Lyme Regis, a village in Dorset on the southern coast of England, where Robinson could devote himself to the only work that really mattered to him:

writing. The outbreak of World War I in August forced them to change their plans.

Still looking for a place where Robinson could write, and with a modest annuity Robinson inherited to support them, they decided to take a friend's advice and visit Carmel-by-the-Sea, a small village nestled in a pine and cypress forest about 275 miles north of Los Angeles. When they arrived in the fall of 1914, only about five hundred people were living there, in cottages set among the trees. A hotel and a handful of stores provided basic services, but there were no paved roads. Main Street, also called Ocean Avenue, ran due west down a hillside in the center of the village to a thin beach shaped like (and, with its pure white sand, as luminous as) a crescent moon. A few miles north lay Monterey, the capital of Alta California during Spanish and Mexican times. Behind the village, rising in the east, were the Sierra de Salinas Mountains. From there, the Carmel River flowed through Carmel Valley as it made its way to the sea. At the mouth of the river stood the picturesque ruins of Misión San Carlos Borromeo del Río Carmelo. Built by Fray Junípero Serra in 1771, the mission once served as headquarters for all the missions on El Camino Real, the road the Spaniards traveled between San Diego and San Francisco. The Santa Lucia Mountains, the Ventana wilderness, and the precipitous cliffs of the incomparable Big Sur marked the coast to the immediate south.

Carmel was already known as an artists' colony when Robinson and Una arrived. George Sterling, a Bohemian poet from San Francisco, built a home in Carmel in 1905 and resided there, off and on, through the spring of 1914. He was at the center of a community of writers who either lived in or visited Carmel. Jack London was one of Sterling's closest friends; others in the group included Mary Austin, Sinclair Lewis, and Upton Sinclair. Painters such as William Merritt Chase and Xavier Martinez were also drawn to Carmel and the surrounding area by the natural beauty they found there and by the opportunity for quiet, uninterrupted work. Actors, dancers, and musicians settled in Carmel as well, attracted by the village's commitment to the performing arts. Some residents were refugees from the business world; others were retired professional men and women; still others were academics from Stanford or Berkeley who lived on Professor's Row. The balance of the population was composed of ordinary people who preferred small-town congeniality, along with assorted independent spirits not quite fit for the conventional world. It was a place for people who wished to live simply, close to nature, and in touch with the elemental forces of life.

The setting was ideal for Robinson and Una. "When the stage-coach topped the hill from Monterey," he recollected later (in a biographical note printed on the jacket of his *Roan Stallion, Tamar and Other Poems*), "and we looked down through pine and sea-fogs on Carmel Bay, it was evident that we had come without knowing it to our inevitable place." As newlyweds still grieving for the loss of their child, they were grateful for the solitude they found in their woodland cabin and for the chance to read, write, and explore the seacoast. Looking back on this fortunate moment in an essay written for the *Carmel Pine Cone* (April 19, 1940), Una describes their life in glowing terms.

So began our happy life in Carmel, full and over full of joy from the first. For a long time we knew no one, but we were busy from morning till night anyway. Robin was writing poetry, his reputation yet to make; I was studying certain aspects of late 18th Century England and receiving from the State Library at Sacramento, through the little village library, priceless packages of old and rare books on my subject. There was housework, and continual woodchopping to fill the maw of the great fireplace in our drafty cabin. We bought simple textbooks on flowers, shells, birds, and stars and used them. We explored the village street by street, followed the traces of the moccasin trail through the forest, and dreamed around the crumbling walls about the old mission. When we walked up from the shore at sunset scarfs of smoke drifting up from hidden chimneys foretold our own happy supper and evening by the fire. It was pleasant to sniff the air and recognize the pungent scent of eucalyptus, the faint, somehow nostalgic quality of burning oak, the gunpowdery smell of driftwood, redwood like ripe apricots, and keener than all, the tonic resin of pitch pine.

A hushed timelessness marked the area. In his foreword to *Selected Poetry* (1938), Jeffers describes the larger setting. "For the first time in my life," he says, "I could see people living— amid magnificent unspoiled scenery—essentially as they did in the Idyls or the Sagas, or in Homer's Ithaca. Here was life purged of its ephemeral accretions. Men were riding after cattle, or plowing the headland, hovered by white sea-gulls, as they have done for thousands of years, and will for thousands of years to come."

Although it might have seemed like they had found Arcadia, Jeffers knew from the outset that Carmel was a dangerous place—dangerous in the way deep love is dangerous, with its wildness, unpredictability, and shattering power. In "Dream of the Future," an early poem addressed to Una, he asks a question that, for the rest of his life, never left his mind: "How do we dare to live / In so great and tameless a land?"

He also wondered how he could dare to write there. In fact, at this time in his life he wondered if he could write at all. In 1912 he published a book of poems at his own expense called *Flagons and Apples*, but he knew the book was little more than a self-indulgent trifle. Since then, he had tried his hand at fiction, publishing a short story titled "Mirrors" in the August 1913 issue of *Smart Set*, but he dismissed that work, too, as undistinguished. By 1914 he had abandoned fiction and returned, once and for all, to poetry, but his new life in Carmel had not yet led to success. It had led, rather, to a deeper awareness of his failure. During a walk in the woods one day that autumn, as Jeffers tells the story in his introduction to *Roan Stallion, Tamar and Other Poems* (Modern Library edition), he struggled with inner turmoil. "I was already a year older than Keats when he died," he remembers thinking, "and I too had written many verses, but they were all worthless. I had imitated and imitated, and that was all."

Some contemporary poets—appearing in *Poetry* (first published in 1912) and other fashionable journals—had found originality by following the principles of Futurism, Imagism, Vorticism, and other avant-garde movements. These poets were riding the crest of a wave that also brought the 1913 International Exhibition of Modern Art to New York. The Armory Show, as it was called, challenged viewers with innovative works such as Duchamp's *Nude Descending a Staircase*, Matisse's *Blue Nude*, Picasso's *Woman with Mustard Pot*, and Kandinsky's *The Garden of Love (Improvisation Number 27)*. In Paris the same year, Stravinsky and Nijinsky excited the worlds of music and ballet with the premiere of their revolutionary *Rite of Spring*.

What Jeffers saw happening in poetry did not look promising—at least for him. "By going farther and farther along the way that perhaps Mallarmé's aging dream had shown them," some poets were breaking new ground by "divorcing poetry from reason and ideas." According to Jeffers, however, by "renouncing intelligibility" they "had turned off the road into a narrowing lane." Further progress could only result from more renunciations: "ideas had gone, now meter had gone, imagery would have to go; then recognizable emotions would have to go; perhaps at last even words might have to go or give up their meaning, nothing be left but musical syllables." The Italian Futurist F. T. Marinetti had already begun to move in that direction with his *Zang Tumb Tuuum* and related works. Other contemporary poets had found originality by employing a technique used by Chinese scholars: "eliminate one's own words from the poem, use quotations from books as the elder poets used imagery from life and nature, make something new by putting together a mosaic of the old." But this route, too, seemed futile. Because he "did not want to become slight and fantastic, abstract and unintelligible" like some poets of his time, Jeffers felt "doomed to go on imitating dead men" unless some impossible wind should blow him "emotions or ideas, or a point of view, or even mere rhythms" that had not yet occurred to others.

Just as he was beginning to confront these issues, and others crucial to his artistic identity, Jeffers received word that his father had had a stroke. He and Una left for Pasadena immediately, but Dr. Jeffers never regained consciousness; he died December 20, 1914, two days after they arrived. Already stricken by the death of his daughter earlier in the year, Jeffers was wounded once again. As 1915 unfolded, grief resulting from his losses, doubt concerning his vocation, and worry about the war in Europe tempered his happiness.

II. TIDES OF FIRE

The tides are in our veins, we still mirror the stars, life is your child,
    but there is in me
Older and harder than life and more impartial, the eye that watched
    before there was an ocean.

That watched you fill your beds out of the condensation of thin vapor
    and watched you change them,
That saw you soft and violent wear your boundaries down, eat rock,
    shift places with the continents.

Mother, though my song's measure is like your surf-beat's ancient
    rhythm I never learned it of you.
Before there was any water there were tides of fire, both our tones flow
    from the older fountain.

Circa 1922—from "Continent's End"

1915–1920

World War I officially ended in 1919—another pivotal moment in modern history. Combat ceased on Armistice Day,
November 11, 1918, but peace was not secured until the Treaty
of Versailles was signed in June the following year. It was an
uneasy peace, the world eventually discovered, but at least
the guns were silenced for a time. As people staggered out
of the darkness and surveyed the damage around them, they

were faced with numbers no one had ever seen: approximately 9,000,000 soldiers and 13,000,000 civilians killed along with at least 30,000,000 wounded or missing; hundreds of thousands of homes and buildings destroyed; whole villages and towns leveled; cities bombed; thousands of square miles of land despoiled; roads, bridges, and railways gone; three empires—Russian, German, Austro-Hungarian—fallen, and a fourth, the Ottoman, crumbling away. Interior landscapes were equally devastated. For millions of demobilized soldiers, along with all the parents, fiancées, wives, and children who lost their loved ones, mental and spiritual scars were deep. Some of the shell-shocked, with minds as barren and beaten as the surface of the moon, never smiled or wept or spoke coherently again.

There was widespread jubilation in Europe in the wake of the war, but even the loudest shouts of happiness were muffled by an overarching experience of despair. For those not previously aware of it, the Death of God had come to pass and civilization seemed to be in ruins. People, sensing the meaninglessness and futility of it all, were appalled by the savagery they saw in themselves and others, a savagery that called into question every notion once held concerning human virtue, the wisdom of leaders, the spirit of brotherhood, and the efficacy of reason. Some artists, such as Tristan Tzara and his fellow Dadaists, dealt with the debacle by focusing on the absurdity of the human condition. Others, like George Grosz, sought to expose mankind's dumb brutality. Oswald Spengler, an independent scholar, provided a naturalistic explanation for recent events in *The Decline of the West*, a book published in Germany as the war drew to a close. Western Civilization, Spengler argued, is an organic entity, doomed, like all other civilizations, to follow the path that leads from birth, growth, and decay to inevitable death.

Americans were proud of the role they played in ending the war, but they, too, were deeply shaken. They had entered the conflict in April 1917, told by President Wilson that American valor was required to "make the world safe for democracy." Of the nearly 5,000,000 men rushed into uniform by conscription or enlistment, about 2,000,000 served overseas, and, of these, over 300,000 were killed or wounded. Compared to English, French, and German casualties, this number was low—but, from the American perspective, it was a high price to pay for a fight that many felt was not their own.

Support for Wilson dropped rapidly after the war, and his dream for a League of Nations failed when Americans turned against it. Furthermore, Americans had more to think about in 1919 than what was happening "over there." The influenza epidemic that began on a military base in Kansas in 1918—and was carried by servicemen across the country, to Europe, and beyond—was still raging. According to government statistics, by the time the illness passed, nearly 900,000 Americans lay dead, along with as many as 50,000,000 (possibly more) victims worldwide.

Retrospective uncertainty about America's involvement in the war and feelings of panic concerning the flu were matched by other tensions and fears in 1919. Labor unrest led to major strikes in Seattle, Chicago, Boston, and many other cities. Racial conflict sparked violent riots in Arkansas, Illinois, Kentucky, Missouri, Nebraska, North Carolina, Tennessee, Washington, D.C., and elsewhere. A Red Scare, fed by worries about the spread of communism, especially following the Bolshevik Revolution in Russia, swept the country from coast to coast. The Espionage and Sedition Acts of 1917 and 1918 provided the legal and cultural framework for attacks against anyone (outsiders, foreigners, pro-German sympathizers, radicals, socialists, communists, freethinkers) who questioned capitalism and the American Way. Palmer Raids, named for Wilson's attorney general, were used to smash the offices of radical labor unions and the headquarters of communist and socialist organizations. Leftists like Emma Goldman were arrested and swiftly driven from the land.

Other factors also contributed to a mood of nervous tension. The tremendous energy committed to the war effort was still pumping through the nation's veins when the war itself suddenly stopped, and that energy—seen in heightened factory production, more women and people of color in the workplace, denser urban populations, greater mobility as more automobiles sped faster along newly made roads, and countless other effects of rapid modernization—could not be damped down. Moreover, the Eighteenth Amendment to the Constitution, which prohibited the manufacture, sale, and transportation of intoxicating beverages, was ratified in 1919, and the Nineteenth Amendment, which gave voting rights to women, was passed by the House and Senate. Old social structures were dissolving as new ones materialized, seemingly shaped on the run.

The years 1915 to 1919 were a gauntlet for Jeffers, too. When he returned to Carmel after the death of his father in December 1914, he and Una resumed their life of reading, writing, and exploring the seacoast. Jeffers experienced an immediate expansion of his powers as a poet. His first major book, *Californians*, was accepted by Macmillan and published in October 1916. It opens with an "Invocation" in *terza rima* and then follows with a character sketch titled "Stephen Brown" in *ottava rima*. The remainder of the book displays a journeyman's command of varied verse forms, rhyme schemes, and meters. Some poems are autobiographical; "The Year of Mourning," for instance, expresses Jeffers' grief over the loss of his father and daughter. Most of the poems are fictional narratives, however, and tell stories about lives shaped by solitude, circumstance, and passion: old men living and dying alone in the mountains; a girl who dances naked in the rain; a brother and sister who fall in love before discovering they are related and who are then tracked down and murdered by an outraged sibling; a child morbidly disturbed by the vision of a white horse rising from the sea; an orphaned doe returned to the wild with a bell around her neck to keep her safe from hunters. While publication of the book vindicated Jeffers' sense of himself as a poet and opened the door to an actual career, it also forced him to reconsider the issue of originality. He knew his work was still rooted in tradition and thus, given advances made by others, overly formal, derivative, and behind the times.

Jeffers' limitations became all the more self-apparent when he attempted to write about World War I in the midst of the tragedy. Fellow poets, like those affiliated with Amy Lowell in *Some Imagist Poets* (1915) and other books, were calling for work that was hard, clear, and concentrated. Use the language of common speech, they said; create new rhythms, render particulars exactly, avoid vague generalities, and desist from cosmic pomposities. Ignoring every aspect of this advice, Jeffers devoted himself to an enormous work titled *The Alpine Christ*. More than two hundred pages of the abandoned manuscript survive—the first portion of a three-part project, Wagnerian in scope, called *Witnesses*.

Jeffers modeled *The Alpine Christ* on big works like Milton's *Paradise Lost*, Shelley's *Prometheus Unbound*, and Hardy's *The Dynasts*. He may have had Wagner's *Ring* cycle in mind as well, for, like *Götterdämmerung*, *The Alpine Christ* is concerned with the twilight of the gods. As the verse drama opens, Satan (who admits to being little more than a jester) spars verbally with Michael and Raphael, his fellow archangels, at the gates of heaven. After an audience with God, wherein a Job-like wager involving world war is made, Satan returns to Earth. God himself sends his Angel of Death to Archduke Francis Ferdinand, whose assassination sparks the conflagration.

As the Great War on Earth unfolds, numerous human and supernatural beings express their bewilderment and pain; among them, in the first act alone, are Elder Angels, Younger Angels, Voices from the Middle Sky, Valkyries, A Voice from the Lower Sky, A File of Spirits, Earthward Spirits, Heavenward Spirits, The Soldier, The King, The Officer, Celestial Witnesses, The Souls of Slain Men, and The Son of God. Out of pity, The Son of God—Christ—goes down to

Earth. He enters and possesses the body of Manuel Rüegg, formerly a thirty-year-old imbecile in Switzerland, and begins to spread a message of peace and love. In the midst of this, also in Switzerland, A Young Man Who Is Mourning His Father (based on Jeffers himself) struggles to understand his personal loss.

Eventually, as war rages, God realizes that he is not in control of events after all—Fate is. He also realizes that he, too, must die. Soon enough, with powers waning and mind unraveling, he passes away, and then "there is blackness / Where glory was." Satan, also fated to disappear, loses strength, repents somewhat, and leaves the scene, "bent and rather tottering." Among the higher powers, this leaves Christ alone on Earth. After releasing the remaining angels from service and dispatching them to oblivion, Christ turns to the world, hoping, all by himself, to stop the fighting and salve human wounds with a message of love. At this point, "an hour climacteric," the drama ends.

Since Jeffers did not complete *Witnesses*, it is impossible to say what might happen next. Given the logic of his story, where Fate rules all, it is likely that Christ—in part an imbecile and, like his Father, blind to his own limitations—would suffer in the same way he suffered before. This time, though, with God already dead and heaven gone, his crucifixion would foreclose all contact with a transcendent, spiritual dimension of existence. Humans would then be left to themselves.

At a time when Ezra Pound had already captured the literary world's attention with "The apparition of these faces in the crowd; / Petals on a wet, black bough"—a complete poem in two lines—and poets like William Carlos Williams were beginning to think about such things as plums in the icebox and red wheelbarrows, Jeffers' flight to the empyrean on the weary wings of Pegasus was outmoded and over-wrought. He knew this himself. A few years later, when an editor asked about *The Alpine Christ*, Jeffers described it as "useless and absurd." And yet, however flawed the poem as a whole might have been, it contains an abundance of striking images and powerful lines; in its cosmic setting, it also reveals the amplitude of Jeffers' tormented response to World War I.

When, in spring 1917, the call for American volunteers was first proclaimed, Jeffers hesitated. With deep roots in the cultural traditions of the principal European antagonists (Germany, France, and England), he may have experienced divided loyalties. He was also thirty years old at the time, married, and, most important, a father. Una had given birth to twin sons, Garth and Donnan, on November 9, 1916. Delivery took place in Pasadena, where Una was attended by the same physician who presided over her previous pregnancy. After several weeks of loving care in the home of Robinson's mother, the new family returned to Carmel, where Robinson and Una leased a larger cottage and surrendered to the demands and joys of parenthood.

When America leapt into action, Jeffers struggled with the issue of enlistment. "I have had rather a bad time of it," he writes in a December 1917 letter to a friend, "between wanting to enter the service and not wanting to afflict my wife. If she had been willing, I could have endured leaving her and the babies; but she did not think there was need of my going. My nerves quite went to pieces from long indecision; I could do my work more or less, but had not an ounce of energy to spend on correspondence." He then adds,

But Una is reconciled now; since Russia's collapse we all have a better understanding of what our country faces. I am filling out an application for training for a commission in the Army Balloon School at Fort Omaha; I don't think myself quite good enough to run an aeroplane. I took my preliminary physical examination yesterday; the local doctor thinks I'll pass muster, I hope the Fort-Omahans agree with him.

As it turned out, Jeffers did not meet the physical requirements for air service, and, despite repeated attempts to move his application forward, he never was accepted. He was still trying to enlist in October 1918, just before armistice was declared. Soon thereafter, as damage done by the war became more widely known and cries for vengeance against the Germans were raised (and then codified in the Treaty of Versailles), Jeffers' feelings hardened into bitter denunciation. "They have all meant well," Jeffers says in "The Truce and the Peace," a sequence of sonnets begun in November, "Our enemies and the knaves at whom we've laughed, / The liars, the clowns in office, the kings in hell." Whatever their intentions, in actual fact, Jeffers realized, the nations' leaders "Conspired, oppressed, robbed, murdered, lied and lied" and, like Pied Pipers, led spellbound millions to their doom. Deluded soldiers thought they "fought for freedom's sake," but freedom, like a forgotten waif, was "starving in a corner" when they marched by.

The "angry tension" Jeffers admits to in this poem remained for several more months. "The Cloud," a poem written around April 1919, speaks of a "broken heart" and a "weak mood"—stemming, probably, from his frustration as a poet and his anguish over the war. "Sudden lightnings" of his spirit could not break through the gloom, nor could the outward renewal in nature that springtime brings: "that weary cloud / Has not been moved; never; nor now is it shaken, / Though the hills laugh April green, and the waters awaken."

Jeffers did not know it at this time, but his life and art were both about to change.

For several years, during their long walks along the coast, Robinson and Una liked to stop and sit on a low hill beside the sea, just south of Carmel village. Huge boulders, which they called the Standing Stones, were strewn about the site there, giving it the appearance of a prehistoric sanctuary like those found in England, Ireland, and Scotland. When the war ended, Robinson and Una bought the site and started making plans for a home. A design, based upon a Tudor barn Una had seen in England, was submitted to a local contractor about the same time "The Cloud" was written; a contract was signed and construction began in late May or early June.

In Gaelic and other ancient languages of the British Isles, the peak of a rocky hill is called a *tor*, so Robinson and Una named their home Tor House. Built of local granite boulders carried up from the shore by horse and wagon, the cottage

5 Sea Road, from future site of Tor House, 1919

was small and sturdy. The front door opened directly into a cozy, wood-paneled living room, with space enough for Una's Steinway grand piano. A kitchen, bath, and guest room completed the downstairs. Two connecting bedrooms—one for the boys and one for Robinson and Una—were up a short flight of stairs, through a trapdoor in the ceiling. The structure was composed as a simple rectangle, oriented in line with the four directions. Windows on all sides offered panoramic views of land and sea. There was running water, but no gas, electricity, or telephone. Light came from kerosene lamps, heat from wood-burning fireplaces.

Construction progressed through the summer of 1919. Desiring to have a hand in building his own home, Jeffers offered his services to the master stonemason. The hard work was just what he needed. As the granite walls rose up and the doors and windows were framed and the roof was covered with redwood shingles, his entire being underwent a transformation. As Una says in an April 1934 letter to Lawrence Clark Powell, based on notes Jeffers himself supplied,

The conflict of motives on the subject of going to war or not was probably one of several factors that, about this time, made the world and his own mind much more real and intense to him. Another factor was the building of Tor House. As he helped the masons shift and place the wind and wave-worn granite I think he realized some kinship with it and became aware of strengths in himself unknown before. Thus at the age of thirty-one there came to him a kind of awakening such as adolescents and religious converts are said to experience.

The awakening was similar to what William Blake describes in *The Marriage of Heaven and Hell*. "Man has closed himself up, till he sees all things thro' narrow chinks of his cavern," Blake says, but "If the doors of perception were cleansed every thing would appear to man as it is, infinite." As Jeffers worked on Tor House, the doors of perception— the fullness of his own poetic consciousness—opened, and the world suddenly (over the course of a summer) became timeless and transparent. "There is in me," he says in "Continent's End," written after his awakening, "Older and harder and more impartial, the eye that watched before there was an ocean." With this eye, Jeffers could see the granite earth when it was molten, before the sea was formed. "Mother," he says, "though my song's measure is like your surf-beat's

6 Tor House, 1919

ancient rhythm I never learned it of you. / Before there was any water there were tides of fire, both our tones flow from the older fountain."

1920—1925

"The world broke in two in 1922 or thereabouts," says Willa Cather in her preface to *Not Under Forty*, a collection of essays. The title of the book, she explains, is like a road sign that contains a warning; in this case, it means that people under forty in 1936 when the book was published would probably not be interested in its contents. Cather's essays are rooted in vanished worlds: memories of a chance encounter and a fleeting friendship with Madame Caroline Grout (a niece of Gustave Flaubert), who talks of music and literature and shares vivid recollections of her uncle and his friends—Turgenev, George Sand, and others; a visit to the widow of an eminent American publisher in her Boston home where Longfellow, Emerson, Whittier, Hawthorne, Dickens, Thackeray, and many other notables were once entertained; reflections on the work of Sarah Orne Jewett, Thomas Mann, and Katherine Mansfield. Sometimes, subtle comments reveal Cather's dismay over changes in the world around her, as when she says, in reference to a hotel she was staying in, "I had set out from the Parker House (the old, the real Parker House, before it was 'modernized')." In other places, she directly addresses the basic issue that bothers her—the loss of contact with the past in favor of contemporaneity and a turn toward the future. "Just how did this change come about," she wonders in one instance. "When and where were the Arnolds overthrown and the Brownings devaluated? Was it at the Marne? At Versailles, when a new geography was being made on paper? Certainly the literary world which emerged from the war used a new coinage. In England and America the 'masters' of the last century diminished in stature and pertinence, became remote and shadowy."

Cather may have overstated her case somewhat. In the aftermath of the war, many artists and intellectuals were, in fact, anxious to raze what remained of the ruined Western tradition and start over. Many others, though, like the owners of the hotel she stayed in, were willing to renovate the old and damaged structure, to bring it back some way. The twin impulses together, along with others that emerged at the same time, produced one of the most remarkable periods of creative activity in human history—not just in literature but in science, technology, and all the arts.

Some call the years 1921 to 1925 *anni mirabili*. For extent of influence and use, the most valuable literary coinage of those years was minted by James Joyce and T. S. Eliot, authors in 1922 of *Ulysses* and *The Waste Land*, respectively. Nothing compares to the impact they had on fiction and poetry, at the time of publication and long after. Between 1921 and 1925, however, many other great writers suddenly appeared and, along with already established authors, published works of enduring value. Examples include F. Scott Fitzgerald, *The Great Gatsby*; Robert Frost, *New Hampshire*, containing "Stopping by Woods on a Snowy Evening" and "Two Look at Two"; Sinclair Lewis, *Babbitt* and *Arrowsmith*; Thomas Mann, *The Magic Mountain*; Eugene O'Neill, *Desire Under the Elms*; Ezra Pound, *Cantos I–XVI*; George Bernard Shaw, *Saint Joan*; Wallace Stevens, *Harmonium*, containing "Sunday Morning" and "Thirteen Ways of Looking at a Blackbird"; William Carlos Williams, *Spring and All*; Virginia Woolf, *Jacob's Room* and *Mrs Dalloway*; and W. B. Yeats, *A Vision* and *Michael Robartes and the Dancer*, containing "The Second Coming."

The exceptional achievements in fiction, poetry, and drama in the early 1920s were matched by pathbreaking work in other arts. Individuality and improvisation were central to the fast tempo, driving rhythm, and earthiness of jazz, the popular and expressionistic music that arose in the southern United States, spread throughout the country, and then made its way to Europe. George Gershwin appropriated the jazz idiom for his *Rhapsody in Blue*. Other composers—such as Ottorino Respighi, Arnold Schoenberg, Dmitri Shostakovich, Igor Stravinsky, and Ralph Vaughan Williams—extended the reach of classical music in different directions. One path led toward experiments with dissonance and atonality.

Pablo Picasso set aside his Cubist explorations for a few years and returned to a traditional figurative mode. In a style called neoclassic, sometimes reminiscent of frescoes found on the walls of villas in ancient Rome, he painted *Woman in White*, *Three Graces*, and additional works. Other artists, unwilling to forsake their commitment to avant-garde iconoclasm, continued their assault against tradition. As Tristan Tzara said at the time, speaking for the Dadaists, "the Beautiful and the True in art do not exist," "everything happens in a completely idiotic way," and "nothing is more delightful than to confuse and upset people." Through the use of found material, random arrangement, obscure content, nonsensical titles, and other techniques, Tzara explains in his "Lecture on Dada," Dadaists sought to "destroy the drawers of the brain and social organization"—or at least make people question their assumptions about art and life and, possibly, make them laugh. Among the noteworthy Dadaist works completed during the years 1921–1925 is Marcel Duchamp's multimedia sculpture, *The Bride Stripped Bare of Her Bachelors, Even*. As Dadaism merged with Surrealism, it resulted in such works as *Two Children Are Threatened by a Nightingale* by Max Ernst. Many painters, preferring abstraction, pursued completely non-objective styles. Examples on the expressive end of the abstract spectrum include *Blue Circle* and *Reminiscence* by Wassily Kandinsky; examples on the rational end include *Composition I with Red, Yellow, and Blue* and *Composition with Yellow, Blue, Black, Red, and Gray* by Piet Mondrian.

The trend toward abstraction, especially the type associated with rationalism, also influenced developments in architecture. Walter Gropius, who founded the Bauhaus in Weimar in 1919 and then moved it to Dessau in 1925, and Le Corbusier, who was based in France, advocated the use of manufactured materials (concrete, steel, and glass) and mass production in the creation of functional buildings in simple, unadorned geometric shapes, with an emphasis on straight lines. Their preference for industrial technology and precision engineering resulted in buildings that were stripped of any reference to cultural

7 Donnan, Una, and Garth Jeffers on Sea Road, ca. 1922

history. Architecture is the "pure creation of the mind," said Le Corbusier in *Towards a New Architecture.*

Jeffers' contribution to the extraordinary work of this period was a book titled *Tamar and Other Poems,* which he published at his own expense in 1924. When this book proved to be a sensation, an expanded trade edition titled *Roan Stallion, Tamar and Other Poems* was rushed into print by New York publishers Boni & Liveright in 1925. Though a few of the poems in these books were written prior to the epiphany Jeffers experienced while building Tor House in 1919, most were written after, and the volume as a whole reveals the thematic concerns, technical mastery, and visionary reach of Jeffers' mature style.

Roan Stallion, the first title poem in the book, tells the story of California, a young woman of mixed race living on an isolated ranch in Carmel Valley with her brutish husband and little daughter. A large, nearly wild stallion won by her husband while gambling is seen by California as the embodiment of divine power. One night, with the ardor of Pasiphae, the woman in Greek mythology who loved a bull, she leaps onto the stallion's back, grips his body with her thighs, and rides "the savage and exultant strength of the world" up a long hill into the moonlit countryside. When the stallion stops to graze, California dismounts and lies at his feet, weeping. She then experiences a spiritual union (an ecstasy similar to that of Saint Teresa as depicted by Bernini) accompanied by mythic revelations. The next evening, California's drunken husband is knocked to the ground by the stallion. California watches as the animal tramples him to death and then, "moved by some obscure human fidelity," shoots the horse three times. As the "beautiful strength" collapses to the ground, she turns a stunned face toward her daughter—"the mask of a woman / Who has killed God."

Tamar, the second title poem, tells the story of the doomed Cauldwells who live in an isolated home on Point Lobos, south of Carmel. The head of the house is David Cauldwell, an old, broken-down man who frequently quotes the Bible. Two children, a son named Lee and a daughter Tamar, live with him, along with his demented sister Jinny, and Stella Moreland, the sister of his dead wife Lily. The action of the story, set around the time of America's entry into World War I, concerns Tamar's incestuous relationship with her brother, an ensuing pregnancy, and her seduction of an unloved suitor to snare a respectable father for the child. Through her Aunt Stella, a medium for the dead, Tamar learns that her father had an incestuous relationship with his sister Helen, which makes her behavior seem more like the simple repetition of a family pattern instead of the singular act of a bounds-breaking free spirit. In the process of coming to terms with this knowledge, Tamar dances naked in a trance-induced frenzy on the seashore, where she is violated by the ghosts of Indians who once lived on Point Lobos, and where she speaks with the ghost of her Aunt Helen, her father's sister-lover. As Tamar's mind sickens, she thinks of ways to destroy her family, especially after learning that her brother, seeking adventure, plans to enlist and leave home. The end comes in a wild conflagration. On the eve of her brother's departure, with her benighted suitor at hand, Tamar orchestrates an explosion of jealous rage. As her brother pulls a knife and stabs her suitor, Tamar's Aunt Jinny sets the house on fire. Floors break, walls fall, and everyone perishes in the flames.

The Tower Beyond Tragedy, a verse drama that follows *Roan Stallion* in the book, presents a condensed version of Aeschylus' *Oresteia*. The action begins when Agamemnon returns home and is met by his wife, Clytemnestra, who is barely able to conceal her long-simmering rage. Agamemnon had left her ten years before to fight the Trojans for Helen, Clytemnestra's beautiful sister. At the outset of the battle, he sacrificed their young daughter Iphigenia so that the Greek fleet could sail. Now, having returned home with Cassandra, a war-prize who is also a prophet, he intends to pick up where he left off as king. Clytemnestra has other plans, however, and kills him the first chance she gets—when Agamemnon, helpless, is taking a bath. But the murder demands vengeance, and the task falls to Orestes, Agamemnon and Clytemnestra's son. Urged on by his sister Electra, Orestes summons the courage to kill his mother. When he does so, a portion of his mind is numbed. In this condition, he also kills Cassandra, and then, slowly, rather than suffering a prolonged attack by the Furies, as in Aeschylus' version, full sanity returns to Orestes, and he achieves a profound state of clarity and calm. His higher state of consciousness (the "Tower Beyond Tragedy" of the title) enables him to see the world and his own action from a new perspective, *sub species aeternitatis*.

In turning to Aeschylus for inspiration, Jeffers reentered one of the principal fountainheads of Western mythology—

the Trojan War, as imagined first by Homer and then by generations of other artists. The particular aspect of the war that Jeffers probed in *The Tower Beyond Tragedy* was the return home of Agamemnon, a subject with particular resonance in the aftermath of World War I, as millions of soldiers traversed the same ground. Also, by projecting his thoughts about recent events onto an archetypal setting, Jeffers reflected on the enigma of war itself and humanity's enduring proclivity for violence.

This theme appears in *Tamar* as well, where Tamar's ne'er-do-well brother, having volunteered for service, looks forward to leaving home for what he imagines will be a thrilling adventure in Europe. The night before his departure, already feeling like more of a man, he struts around with spurs on. Excited by the mere thought of going to war, cock-sure and jingling as he walks, he arms himself with a whip and a knife, both of which are soon put to use—the whip in a savage attack against his sister, the knife to kill her lover. Like *The Tower Beyond Tragedy*, *Tamar* also draws upon a principal fountainhead of Western mythology: in this case, the stories of depravity and family intrigue found in the Old Testament. In Genesis 38:1–30, Tamar's namesake is a twice-widowed woman who poses as a prostitute and seduces her father-in-law in order to remind him of his continuing obligation to her. In 2 Samuel 13:1–29, Tamar is the maiden daughter of King David who is raped by one brother, Amnon, and avenged by another, Absalom. Soon after these incidents, Absalom turns on his father and then dies in a failed coup d'état. Although *Roan Stallion* does not address the issue of war directly, it does examine the interplay of passion and violence at the heart of human life and culture. *Roan Stallion* also shares something else with the other narratives: an interest in the human psyche at its most transgressive. California, Tamar, and Clytemnestra, along with Cassandra, Electra, Orestes, and other characters, are driven by forces within themselves that push them far beyond the reach of conventional morality.

In addition to these three major works, *Roan Stallion, Tamar and Other Poems* contains another long narrative, a sonnet sequence, an idyll, and over thirty lyric poems of varying length. Altogether, the book probes a wide variety of topics, including, along with those mentioned above, the primacy of silence and darkness in the universe, which ultimately overtakes all sound and light; the sublime beauty and supreme indifference of nature; the specious wisdom of spiritual leaders, specifically that of Christ and the Buddha; Jeffers' understanding of himself as a man and poet; the unique place of California in American life and in Western Civilization as a whole; and the dangers facing America, especially those brought on by pretensions to empire. For most of the poems (except those bound by convention, like the sonnets), Jeffers uses a line composed of syllable-based rhythmic stresses. Rhythms, tied to subject matter, vary from poem to poem and derive, as Jeffers says in a note based on a July 3, 1927 letter, from "physics—biology—the beat of blood, the tidal environments of life" and from "a desire for singing emphasis that prose does not have." Some of his lines are short, others quite long—as many as twenty-five syllables in length—but all are carried by a cadence that is unforced and natural, like the steady breaking of waves upon the shore. Diction is natural, too, as is syntax. Unlike many other poets of his time who relied on feints and dodges to achieve their aims (through irony, ambiguity, obscurity, fragmentation, and other means), Jeffers speaks directly to his readers. He hoped to share, in no uncertain terms, all that he had learned—or, better said, all that he was learning, for, as he continued his work as a stonemason, his heart remained open to the sea and sky.

After Tor House itself was completed, and after Jeffers had learned enough to work by himself with stone, he proceeded to build a garage, a pedestal for a sundial, a courtyard wall, and then the incomparable Hawk Tower. The latter project engaged him from 1920 to 1925, the exact years he was working on the majority of the poems published in *Roan Stallion, Tamar and Other Poems.* The tower was completed, except for finishing touches like the paving stones in the lowest room, around the middle of September 1925. Assuming it took a few more weeks to accomplish whatever tasks remained, Hawk Tower was ready for use in November, precisely when his Boni & Liveright book appeared.

Hawk Tower was inspired by the ancient towers of Ireland but designed according to the dictates of Jeffers' own imagination, urged on by Una. It was named for a hawk that circled overhead during construction and alighted on the stones from time to time. To build the structure, Jeffers hauled boulders up from the shore, some weighing nearly 400 pounds, mixed the mortar himself, and set them into

8 Hawk Tower, 1924

place. As the walls rose, he rolled the stones up inclined planks; when this was no longer possible, he used a block-and-tackle system. When finished, the structure was nearly 40 feet high. It contained a "dungeon," a main room on the ground level, a second-story room paneled in mahogany, a third-floor open battlement, and a fourth-floor open turret. A sheltered staircase on the outside of the tower connects all four floors. The two lower floors are also connected by a twisting, hidden staircase built inside the walls, some of which are 6 feet thick.

Jeffers worked on the tower every afternoon. In the evening, following dinner, he would sit by the fire in Tor House and read aloud to Una and the twins. Before going to bed, he stepped outside to breathe the ocean air, study the stars, and collect his thoughts for the next day's work. In the morning, he paced and wrote upstairs. After several hours devoted to poetry, he came down for lunch. By mid-afternoon, he was back at work on the tower. And so it went, day after day, with writing and stonemasonry bound together in a mutually stimulating round.

The granite boulders Jeffers used to construct Hawk Tower, like those used for Tor House, were millions of years old. Jeffers was mindful of this as he set them into place. Along with these sea-rounded boulders, Jeffers cemented stones from around the world into both structures—some collected by Una and himself, others provided by friends; some in their natural state, others worked by human hands. Examples include a meteorite fragment, lava from Mt. Vesuvius, petrified wood, assorted mineral samples, stones from prehistoric cairns in the British Isles, pieces of the Great Pyramid of Cheops in Egypt, a tile inscribed with a cuneiform prayer to Ishtar from the Babylonian Temple of Erech, a carving from the Angkor temples in Cambodia, a piece of the Great Wall of China, a carved human torso from India, terra-cotta heads and an obsidian dagger from Central America, tiles from the Baths of Caracalla in Rome, a fragment of a painted plaque from the ruins of Pompeii, carved marble from the island of Delos in Greece, stones from the sites of round towers in Ireland, tile from Kenilworth Castle in England, a stone from Lord Byron's home, arrowheads, and stonework from several California missions.

Artifacts within Tor House and Hawk Tower were equally resonant. Robinson and Una were not collectors and neither liked clutter, but they enjoyed having things around them that had stories to tell. Family heirlooms—like a spinning wheel, oil lamps dating from before the Civil War, and a Wedgwood vase—could be found in each room, along with items discovered in antique shops, handmade furniture, and gifts from friends, such as a frame containing leaves from the trees shading Shelley's grave in Rome. Naturally inclined toward the principles of the Arts and Crafts movement, Robinson and Una followed William Morris' dictum: "Have nothing in your house that you do not know to be useful, or believe to be beautiful."

The Arts and Crafts movement flourished in California from approximately 1895 to 1920. In rustic places like Carmel, where "modern art" at the latter end of that period (and for many years beyond) meant plein-air impressionism, it lasted longer. Charles Sumner Greene, the noted architect who, with his brother Henry, designed the Gamble House in Pasadena and other Arts and Crafts masterpieces, moved to Carmel in 1916. His last major commission, the D. L. James House, built of native stone and perched on a cliff in the Carmel Highlands, was completed in 1922. Greene, like others inclined toward the Arts and Crafts philosophy, valued unity and simplicity in design, respect for vernacular traditions, harmony with nature, the use of local materials, minimal ornamentation, handcraftsmanship, and warm, domestic interiors. As a mystic who studied theosophy and Eastern wisdom, Greene believed that architecture springs from, and should inspire, the creative human soul.

Without thinking about it, Jeffers shared this conviction. Building Tor House and Hawk Tower was an intuitive enterprise, rooted in instinct and compelled by inner necessity. Even such decisions as the basic design for Tor House— a Tudor barn—had hidden logic, especially for a poet like Jeffers. The Tudor period in England, ranging from 1485 to 1603, spans the years of the Northern Renaissance. King Henry VIII and Queen Elizabeth lived during that time, as did Edmund Spenser, Sir Philip Sidney, Christopher Marlowe, William Shakespeare, Ben Jonson, and other poets. By building a home in a style these poets could recognize, where he dedicated himself to writing poetry they all could understand, Jeffers made himself one with his literary ancestors and honored, in stone and verse, the cultural tradition he and they shared. The hidden logic of Hawk Tower, insofar as design is concerned, was more atavistic. In the way it rises from the earth with self-sufficient grandeur, it looks pre-medieval—like a stronghold built by a Celtic chieftain in the remote Dark Ages.

Carl Jung would have understood the structure, as well as Jeffers' need to build it. He himself purchased property on Lake Zurich in 1922 where, the following year, he began work on a tower named for the nearby village—Bollingen. As he expanded his tower through the 1920s and beyond, it anchored his creative life and became for him a place of discovery and transformation. W. B. Yeats would have understood Hawk Tower, too, for he was living in his own tower at this time, Thoor Ballylee in County Galway. Yeats moved into the property with his family in 1919, but restoration of the ancient structure continued for the next few years. Along with the simultaneity of their tower-building, Jeffers, Jung, and Yeats shared other concerns. All three were interested in the deep structures of human consciousness, especially the role played by symbols and myths in individual and communal life; each developed a comprehensive system to explain and mitigate the interplay of creative and destructive forces in human behavior; and each, following World War I, looked at the immediate past with horror and the future with foreboding.

Yeats, in "The Second Coming," expresses some of the anxiety experienced by all three during this crucial moment in history. "Things fall apart; the centre cannot hold," he says, "Surely some revelation is at hand." Portending danger, he wonders "what rough beast, its hour come round at last, / Slouches towards Bethlehem to be born?" In the highly charged political atmosphere following the war, more than one such creature with "a gaze blank and pitiless as the sun" was coming into view. Mussolini took control of Italy in 1922; Stalin was appointed general secretary of the Central Committee of the Russian Communist Party in the same year; and, in 1925, Adolf Hitler published *Mein Kampf*.

1925–1930

There is a scene near the end of *The Odyssey* when Odysseus, having returned home disguised as a beggar, takes stock of the suitors who are selfishly eating his food and harassing his wife. Suddenly, the suitors start laughing; they laugh until it hurts, until they bleed, and they keep on laughing—not because something is funny, but because Athena has cast a spell on them and they cannot do otherwise. For as long as the fit lasts, the suitors are terrified, but when it stops, they return to their stolen feast as if nothing happened. A seer in the room knows for certain they are doomed.

In some ways, America in the Roaring Twenties was filled with that kind of forced laughter. Speakeasies pouring bootleg liquor, flappers dancing the Charleston, modish women wearing cloche hats over bobbed hair, flagpole sitting, raccoon coats, movie stars and sports heroes, mah-jongg, crossword puzzles—these and many other fads of the time reveal a certain giddiness, even a frenzy, that became more and more pronounced as Black Tuesday, October 29, 1929, drew nigh. By that time, stock market values were inflated far beyond reason, real estate prices in places like Florida were soaring, and goods were being produced across the country as if demand would always outpace supply.

By 1927, two thirds of American homes had electric power, which resulted in a profusion of "must have" inventions to employ it, such as irons, vacuum cleaners, washing machines, radios, and refrigerators, many of which were bought on credit. A whole new consumer-based, mass-produced culture was emerging, fueled by coast-to-coast advertising campaigns and high-pressure sales. By the end of the decade, with nearly 30,000,000 automobiles on American roads along with millions of trucks and buses, highways lined with billboards stretched in all directions; roadside restaurants, motels, and gas stations were popping up everywhere; and suburban housing developments were blurring the distinction between city and country life. In ways never imagined before, people were on the move.

Carmel was changing, too. With the increase in automobiles came an increase in tourism, and Carmel provided a prime setting for vacationers. Carmel's national reputation as an artists' colony was established early on by word of mouth and by newspaper articles such as "Hotbed of Soulful Culture, Vortex of Erotic Erudition: Carmel in California, Where Author and Artist Folk Are Establishing the Most Amazing Colony on Earth" (*Los Angeles Times*, May 22, 1910), "Carmel: The Land of Unsuppressed Desires" (*New York Tribune*, January 1, 1922), and "Carmel, The Secret Garden of the Gods" (*New York Herald Tribune*, September 19, 1926). With access made easier by the automobile, people were anxious to see the village for themselves and to enjoy its many charms.

One of the individuals who helped make Carmel a tourist destination was Teddie Kuster, Una's first husband and lifelong friend. In 1918 and 1919, as his marriage to Edith was ending, Teddie spent more of his time on artistic pursuits. He eventually closed his law practice in Los Angeles and, having visited Carmel many times, decided to settle there permanently. In December of 1920 he purchased more than an acre of land near Robinson and Una's property. Over the next few months he immersed himself in a variety of local activities. When construction of Teddie's French Norman stone home was completed, he and his third wife, Ruth, became Robinson and Una's nearest neighbors. In 1922 and 1923, Teddie designed and built three shops, each in the old-world European style that became one of Carmel's trademarks.

In 1924 Teddie completed his most ambitious and important project, the construction of the Theatre of the Golden Bough, believed by some to be one of the most beautiful and technically advanced venues of its kind in America. In addition to the plays that Teddie acted in, directed, and produced there, the Theatre of the Golden Bough provided a stage for productions directed by Maurice Browne, an eminent professional from England. It also functioned as the center for a drama school and as an auditorium for vocal and dance recitals, chamber concerts, poetry readings, lectures, and art films from Europe—exactly the kinds of events that appealed to local residents and drew visitors to the town. For more and more tourists, a perfect day in Carmel included a few hours at the beach; lunch at Sally's, the Studio, or the

Blue Bird Tea Room; a stroll through the Corner Cupboard, Seven Arts, Cabbages and Kings, Jasmine Bush, the Wishing Well, Tilly Polak's, and many other small galleries and shops; dinner at Whitney's, Romylane's, or another cozy restaurant; a performance at the Golden Bough; and then a good night's sleep at the La Playa Hotel or the Pine Inn.

Because of Carmel's many attractions, the population more than quadrupled between 1920 and 1929, and as the village grew, so did Robinson and Una's circle of friends. Among the visitors from the San Francisco area who came to Carmel for a few days at a time and who Robinson and Una always liked to see were Dr. Hans Barkan, chairman of the Department of Ophthalmology at Stanford University, and his wife Phoebe; Sara Bard Field and Charles Erskine Scott Wood, writers and social activists; Albert Bender, businessman, art patron, and philanthropist; and the poet George Sterling. Some close friends rented or bought vacation homes and remained in Carmel for weeks or even months at a time. Among them were Frederick ("Timmie") and Maud Clapp, Blanche and Russell Matthias, and Ralph and Jane Whitehead. Timmie Clapp, soon to be named the founding director of the Frick Collection in New York, was a professor of fine arts at the University of Pittsburgh, the author of important studies of Pontormo, and an accomplished poet. Blanche Matthias, originally from Chicago, was an art critic and friend of Georgia O'Keeffe; she and her husband Russell, a businessman, enjoyed world travel. Ralph and Jane Whitehead, both of whom had studied with John Ruskin in their native England, were Arts and Crafts advocates who divided their time between their Carmel and Montecito homes in California, and Byrdcliffe, their estate, workshop, and teaching institution in Woodstock, New York.

Robinson and Una also had many friends among the increasing numbers of people who, like themselves at one time, came to Carmel for a visit, fell in love with the locale, and then purchased property there. Some friends among the recent arrivals were very wealthy. Sidney and Olga Fish, both from prominent New York families, purchased several thousand acres of land overlooking Carmel Valley. Their ranch, called Palo Corona, featured a large home where they entertained visiting celebrities, family, and friends—including Robinson and Una. Olga's sister Sara and her husband Gerald Murphy were doing something similar on the French Riviera, where their home, Villa America, was the meeting place for European and expatriate artists such as Pablo Picasso, Ernest Hemingway, and F. Scott Fitzgerald. Another wealthy couple who lived nearby was George Gordon Moore and his wife Esther. Moore, a financier and champion polo player, was a man with a hidden past; one rumor identified him as an illegitimate son of England's King Edward VII. Esther was the daughter of a former governor of Massachusetts. Their ranch, contiguous in places to Palo Corona, eventually covered over 20,000 acres of land.

Additional friends among the recent arrivals, such as Lincoln Steffens and his wife Ella Winter, were well-off but not exceptionally so. Steffens, who gained fame as a muckraking journalist, was the author of *The Shame of the Cities*, among other books. While writing his *Autobiography*

9 Una Jeffers, 1927

in Carmel, he also contributed columns to the *Carmelite*, a local newspaper, and to *Pacific Weekly*, a journal published in Carmel but distributed more widely. For the latter, he also served as associate editor and then editor. Since Steffens and his wife both leaned politically to the far left, their work in Carmel added new weight to the village's reputation as a haven for radicals and socialists, first acquired in the days of George Sterling and his friends; this helped counterbalance Carmel's growing fame as a stylish retreat for the sophisticated upper class.

Close friends were always welcome at Tor House. As the number of visitors to Carmel increased, however, Robinson and Una redoubled their efforts to secure privacy. They planted a forest of trees around their home and hung a sign on their front gate. On one side, the sign said "NOT AT HOME BEFORE 4:00 P.M."; on the other, "NOT AT HOME." Meanwhile, Jeffers continued to write in the morning, work outdoors in the afternoon, and read aloud by the fire in the evening. By adhering to this regimen, he published three more books in the latter half of the decade: *The Women at Point Sur* (1927), *Cawdor and Other Poems* (1928), and *Dear Judas and Other Poems* (1929).

Of the three, *The Women at Point Sur* (1927) was perhaps the most challenging for readers. As the long narrative opens, the Rev. Dr. Barclay tells his parishioners he can no longer preach the gospel and he is leaving the church. "Christianity is false," he declares one Sunday morning. "The fable that Christ was the son of God and died to save you, died and lived again. Lies." Barclay then steps down from the pulpit and walks out the door, leaving his wife and daughter and a stunned congregation behind. The year is 1919; Barclay is fifty years old; and he is still grieving over the recent loss of his only son, Edward, killed in the Great War. After stopping in Monterey to collect his scattered thoughts, Barclay begins a solitary sojourn southward in pursuit of truth. He walks, delusional at times, until he reaches an isolated farmhouse at Point Sur where he arranges to pay for lodging.

The home is owned by old man Morhead, who lies crippled in an upstairs room. His daughter-in-law, Natalia, manages the property and cares for her little daughter while awaiting the return of her husband, Randal, who left to fight in the war. In his absence, a young woman named Faith Heriot has moved into the house and into Randal's bed. Natalia does not know that Faith and Randal were having an affair prior to his sudden enlistment and that Faith ended a pregnancy by having an abortion. Barclay begins preaching a new religion to Natalia, Faith, and the hired help—a religion based on the presumption that God's commandments are abrogated and everyone is free.

Wishing to live according to his teaching, Barclay pays an Indian serving-woman for sex. By the time Barclay's wife Audis and his daughter April arrive at the farmhouse, hoping to bring him home, Barclay believes he is the prophet of a wild, tormented God—that he is, in fact, the lawless God himself. Flush with feelings of limitless power, he rapes his daughter. April's own sanity is lost as a consequence, and, believing herself to be her dead brother Edward, she tries to shoot her father but turns the gun on herself instead.

While all this is happening, Randal—the returning warrior—arrives home. Confronted with two women he does not love (his wife and his mistress who, themselves, are in the midst of an affair), and suddenly interested in April (just prior to her suicide), he is in turns confused, hostile, and fawning. As tension increases in the home and on the hillside where Barclay preaches, Randal uncovers the relationship between Natalia and Faith, Natalia learns of the affair between Faith and Randal, a fight ensues, Natalia murders her daughter, old man Morhead dies, and Randal runs away screaming in despair. Eventually, Barclay, lost in his fantasy of power, reaches into a fire with both hands and grabs a heap of red coals. He then flees northward until he reaches the mouth of an abandoned coal mine where, still believing himself God, he lies down, dying.

The Women at Point Sur was published in the same year as Sinclair Lewis' *Elmer Gantry* and a year after Aimee Semple McPherson, the celebrated evangelist, was accused of hiding out with a lover in Carmel while pretending to be kidnapped. Jeffers' narrative, however, was not concerned with immorality and hypocrisy in the church. Rather, the epic poem represented another attempt to probe the effect of the Great War on individual Americans, to explore the dynamics of religious enthusiasm (both from the perspective of the charismatic founder of a cult and from that of his ecstatic followers), to place in the mind of a deranged person some of Jeffers' own sincerely held convictions, and to recount the actual torments he perceived in people living on the coast. In regard to the latter, as Jeffers says in an April 24, 1926 letter, "Someone said to me lately that it is not possible to be quite sane here, many others feel a hostility of the region to common human life. Immigration overpowers a place, at least for a while, but where the coast is thinly peopled it seems really to have a mood that both excites and perverts its people." While Jeffers also says the psychology of his stories "was observed from life, and in this country," his narratives are not simply realistic nor local. Through the presence of literary references, symbolism, and archetypal elements, they rise above the mundane and draw their power from the timeless realm of myth.

The title poem of *Cawdor and Other Poems* (1928), for instance, tells the story of another fifty-year-old man, a rancher in the Big Sur named Cawdor. After a nineteen-year-old girl named Fera Martial shows up at his ranch with her blind father, having been driven from their home by a fire, Cawdor offers to take her in. He soon falls in love with her and asks her to marry him. She accepts, only because she and her father have nowhere else to go. When Cawdor's son Hood, a hunter, returns to the ranch, Fera's attention turns to him. Hood rebuffs her repeated advances, and before long her desire turns to anger and she seeks revenge. After Hood leaves the ranch, Fera tells her husband that Hood raped her. Overwhelmed with jealousy and rage, he tracks his son and kills him. When he eventually learns the truth—that Hood was innocent all along—he tries to hide his guilt and stifle his remorse. Before long, the strain becomes too great for him to bear; he tells a hired hand to notify the authorities, and then, still suffering, he picks up a sharpened piece of flint and gouges out his eyes.

Cawdor's story, set within the rugged terrain of the Big Sur, unfolds as a convincing local tragedy. The plot itself, however, derives from Greek mythology, where Phaedra provokes her husband Theseus to kill his son Hippolytus because of the latter's unwillingness to make love to her. Desire, rejection, and false accusation also figure in the biblical story of Joseph and Potiphar's wife. Other associations include Cawdor's name, which links him to Macbeth, Thane of Cawdor; his violent, easily manipulated jealousy, which he shares with Othello; his self-inflicted blindness, prefigured in the act of Oedipus; and, in the case of Hood, a wound in the thigh that connects him to Attis and the priests of Cybele.

Dear Judas and Other Poems (1929) contains two long poems, *Dear Judas* and *The Loving Shepherdess*, and several short lyrics. *Dear Judas* was written at a time of Christian revivalism in America. The *Tennessee v. John Scopes* "Monkey Trial," which set the biblical view of creation against Darwin's theory of evolution, occurred in 1925, and books like Giovanni Papini's *The Life of Christ* and Bruce Barton's *The Man Nobody Knows* were enormous best sellers. Jeffers countered conventional pieties with a verse drama about Jesus' self-delusion and limitless thirst for power.

The frame for *Dear Judas* comes from the Japanese Noh tradition, where spirits reenact a significant event in their lives. In *Dear Judas,* the spirits belong to Judas, Jesus, Mary, and Lazarus, each of whom is compelled to return to the scene of Jesus' passion. As they relive the moment, we learn that Jesus' false dream of greatness is rooted in his belief that he is the Son of God. The delusion originated with his mother, who could not bear to tell him the truth about his actual, illegitimate origin. We also learn that Judas betrayed Jesus in order to protect him and the Jews of Jerusalem from Roman persecution; he thought the authorities would simply arrest his tormented friend and hold him in jail for a few days, not crucify him. Jesus welcomes martyrdom, however, because he knows it will lead to worship and, through blind faith in him, to lasting dominion. "No man shall live / As if *I* had not lived," he says, with a megalomania similar to that of Rev. Barclay in *The Women at Point Sur*. His goal is not just power over people but complete conquest—body, mind, and soul: "To be with my people, / In their very hearts, a part of their being, inseparable from those that love me, more closely touching them / Than the cloth of the inner garment touches the flesh. That this is tyrannous / I know, that it is love run to lust: but I will possess them."

A different side of the Christ archetype is explored in *The Loving Shepherdess*, Jeffers' long narrative about Clare Walker, a young woman who wanders alone through the Big Sur with a dwindling flock of sheep. Clare is based on a character described in a footnote to *The Heart of Midlothian* by Sir Walter Scott. Her name also makes reference to Saint Clare, the follower of Saint Francis of Assisi and founder of the Order of Poor Ladies, a community of nuns also called the Poor Clares. In Jeffers' poem, Clare Walker is doomed by pity and selfless love. Pregnant with a child she knows she cannot deliver (having been told by a doctor that her pelvis is misshapen), she makes her way through the countryside. Threadbare and starving, she offers kindness to everyone she meets, expecting nothing in return, until a day in April when the sharp pains come and she lies down in a willow thicket to die.

The shorter lyrics in *Dear Judas and Other Poems*, like those in previous books, express Jeffers' deepening distrust of human civilization in general and American culture in particular. "The Broken Balance" begins with a reference to a passage in Plutarch's biography of Sulla (Chapter VII) where a trumpet blast is heard in the heavens. Soothsayers interpret the sound as a signal indicating the end of an age and the beginning of a new one. Sulla himself, as he fought his way to power, helped end the republic and prepare the way for empire. In "The Broken Balance," Jeffers admits to hearing just such a sound, a "shrill and mournful" trumpet-blast, which he, too, interprets as a signal of change. Looking to the future, like the prophets in Sulla's day or like Homer's seer who foresaw the suitors' doom, Jeffers descries trouble ahead, beginning with the concentration of power in dictatorial hands and including a world of material abundance where people sell themselves "for toys and protection"— for little more, that is, than fast cars, loud radios, and an arsenal of big guns. As a result, the "uneasy and fractional people" already seem lost. Insulated from nature, trapped in a man-made reality, which is nothing but a hall of mirrors, they have no function but to serve a commercialized, industrialized, and increasingly militarized civilization. "No wonder," Jeffers says, "they live insanely, and desire / With their tongues, progress; with their eyes, pleasure; with their hearts, death."

As he considers the human condition and the deleterious effects of modern life, Jeffers mourns "the broken balance, the hopeless prostration of the earth / Under men's hands and their minds, / The beautiful places killed like rabbits to make a city, / The spreading fungus, the slime-threads / And spores"—his "own coast's obscene future." He takes comfort, however, in knowing that human dominion will not last forever. Looking farther ahead, Jeffers sees "the last man dying / Without succession under the confident eyes of the stars." When this occurs, when humanity—"a moment's accident" in the vast scheme of things—disappears, Earth will recover its "old lonely immortal / Splendor." Referring in "Hooded Night" to the granite cliffs of the Carmel headlands, cliffs that were already millions of years old when the Egyptians built pyramids, Jeffers says "Here is reality. / The other is a spectral episode; after the inquisitive animal's / Amusements are quiet: the dark glory."

Jeffers submitted the finished manuscript of *Dear Judas and Other Poems* to his publisher in May 1929, just before embarking on a trip to the British Isles. He and Una—primarily Una—planned a trip for the family that could last up to a year. As it turned out, seven months was long enough to be away from home. Leaving Tor House by train in early June, the family stopped in Michigan to visit Una's relatives and then continued on to Montreal, where they boarded a ship that took them up the St. Lawrence, across the Atlantic, to Ireland. After purchasing an automobile in Belfast, they leased a cottage in Knocknacarry, County Antrim. With this as their base, the Jeffers family spent nearly three months

10   Tor House and Hawk Tower, ca. 1927

traversing the countryside—visiting villages, ruins, round towers, prehistoric monuments, and other special sites, including those made famous by W. B. Yeats and other writers. They explored every county in Ireland except Wexford, driving 5,000 miles in all.

In September they crossed over to Scotland and continued their sightseeing up through Robert Burns country to John O' Groats in the far north and the Hebrides Islands. From there they drove south, visiting Edinburgh, Melrose, and the country estate of Sir Walter Scott. Reaching England, they passed through the Lake District, home to Wordsworth and Coleridge, and then Yorkshire, where Charlotte and Emily Brontë had lived. Traveling down through the Midlands and the Cotswolds, they eventually reached London where, on an afternoon in mid-October, they had tea with Jeffers' publishers in England, Leonard and Virginia Woolf. A cottage in Oxfordshire provided a base for excursions in central and southern England—home to the builders of Stonehenge, the legendary King Arthur, Shakespeare, and Thomas Hardy.

In late November, just as *Dear Judas* reached bookstore shelves, the Jefferses turned north again and drove through Wales on their way back to Scotland. From there, they returned to Ireland, where they revisited a few favorite places, sold their car (now with 10,000 miles on the odometer), and sailed for home. After a return visit to Michigan, they made their way to Carmel via New Orleans and Los Angeles, arriving at Tor House December 31, 1929.

While Robinson, Una, and the twins were away, the American economy began to behave erratically. Off and on from May to September, there were signs of trouble in the stock market, where individuals and businesses were investing both actual earnings and, through the purchase of stocks on margin, money they did not have. The giddy round of getting and spending that characterized the 1920s had convinced just about everyone that cash registers would keep ringing, and stock values would continue to soar.

When the market crashed in October, with stocks losing nearly 40 percent of their value in just a few days, Americans were stunned. Among the wealthy, family fortunes evaporated; in the middle class, life savings disappeared. Day by day, more businesses closed and banks collapsed. In his State of the Union address, delivered to Congress December 3, 1929, President Hoover dismissed "unwarranted pessimism and fear." "The problems with which we are confronted," he said, "are the problems of growth and progress." He believed the crisis had passed, the economy was under control, and, with a few prudent adjustments, business in America would "continue as usual." He was wrong, of course. The Great Depression had just begun.

III. THE WHIRLWIND'S HEART

Yet it is right that a man's views be expressed, though the poetry suffer for it. Poetry should represent the whole mind; if part of the mind is occupied unhappily, so much the worse. And no use postponing the poetry to a time when these storms have passed, for I think we have but seen a beginning of them; the calm to look for is the calm at the whirlwind's heart.

Circa 1941—from the preface to *Be Angry at the Sun*

1930—1935

"This *is* the most beautiful spot we know," said Una in a letter to a friend after returning home. As much as she and Robinson loved the British Isles, especially the remote and rugged coastal areas, no other place could compare to Tor House and their own rocky shore. With the publication of each successive book by Jeffers, however, privacy eroded. Tourists now regularly walked to Carmel Point or drove there, wanting to see where Jeffers lived; visiting writers and celebrities also hoped to meet him; and Carmel friends regularly knocked on Robinson and Una's door, often bringing invitations to picnics, dinner parties, and other social events.

The months after their return from Europe were especially busy and set a pace that proved typical for years to come. At the end of January, for instance, Albert Bender brought Edna St. Vincent Millay and her husband Eugen

Boissevain to Tor House for a visit. A few days later, Max Eastman passed through Carmel and stopped by. In the area for longer stays were Sinclair Lewis and his wife Dorothy Thompson, and Mabel Dodge Luhan and her husband Tony. Lewis, who would receive the Nobel Prize later in the year, had taken a home in Monterey for February and March. From there, he ventured forth to call on Lincoln Steffens, the MacGowan sisters, and other old friends. On one such excursion, he and Dorothy visited Robinson and Una. At the same time, Mabel Luhan was residing in Carmel, having leased a home across the hollow from Robinson and Una, virtually next door. While the bonds formed with these visitors were cordial and, in some cases, deep—Millay, for instance, hung a framed photograph of Jeffers on a wall in her study and championed his poetry for the rest of her life—the one established with Mabel Luhan proved most consequential.

Mabel was a collector, a trophy hunter of sorts, whose prey was people. Born in Buffalo, New York in 1879, Mabel was the pampered daughter of Charles and Sara Ganson, themselves the indulged children of wealthy socialites. Mabel's first husband was Karl Evans; she pursued him mainly to keep him from marrying a young woman she did not like who lived in her own exclusive neighborhood. They had one child, a son named John, who was born shortly before Karl died in a hunting accident. Prior to John's birth, Mabel had begun an affair with her gynecologist (who may have been John's father); wishing to avoid a major scandal, she left Buffalo for an extended stay in Europe.

In Paris she met Edwin Dodge, a well-to-do Bostonian, who soon became her second husband—even though she told him, candidly, that no romantic feelings were involved. When the couple moved to Florence and purchased the Villa Curonia, a grand estate built by the Medici in the 1400s, Mabel discovered a way of life that suited her. With unlimited means at her disposal and with, conveniently, a husband who was a trained architect, she helped restore the villa to its Renaissance splendor. In turbans and flowing gowns, she attended to all the details of decoration as she sought, desperately at times, to find and express her own inner spirit. For help in this endeavor, she surrounded herself with brilliant people from the worlds of theater, music, and art—among them, Bernard Berenson, Robert de la Comandine, Gordon Craig, Muriel and Paul Draper, Eleanor Duse, André Gide, Arthur Rubinstein, and Gertrude and Leo Stein. In a work that helped make both of them famous, Gertrude Stein captured this phase of Mabel's life in "The Portrait of Mabel Dodge at the Villa Curonia" (1912).

When, soon enough, the Italian Renaissance phase became tiresome, Mabel moved on. She returned to the United States and, wiping out the cloying past with a white decorating scheme, installed herself in a Greenwich Village apartment in New York City, at Washington Square. As she sought ways to deal with inner conflicts and, simultaneously, to change her external world, she reached out once again to artists and intellectuals, which meant—given the extraordinary talent concentrated in New York—connecting with some of the finest minds of the time. In 1913 Mabel helped plan the First Exhibition of Modern Art (also called the Armory Show) and the Paterson Strike Pageant, both of which signaled the dawn of a new, revolutionary spirit in America. More important, she established a salon—one of the most famous in American history. On a given Wednesday or Thursday night, and sometimes more than once a week, dozens of people from all walks of life and political persuasion gathered in Mabel's apartment for debate, conversation, and a midnight meal. An abbreviated list of participating luminaries would include A. A. Brill, Max Eastman, Emma Goldman, Walter Lippmann, Georgia O'Keeffe, John Reed, Edwin Arlington Robinson, Margaret Sanger, Lincoln Steffens, and Alfred Stieglitz. Having long since abandoned her husband, Mabel entered an open affair with John Reed. When this ended, she continued her search for happiness through psychotherapy, mind cure, a move to the country, and, following her official divorce from Dodge, remarriage in 1917 to the artist Maurice Sterne.

Mabel's third marriage foundered right from the start, perhaps because she asked her new husband to take a honeymoon trip without her. Not long after his return, she planned another trip for him, this time to Santa Fe, New Mexico. When she eventually followed him there, she did not like what she saw. Soon, though, the austere beauty of the area overcame her, and, when she ventured up the Sangre de Cristo Mountains to the remote village of Taos, she completely lost her heart. Here, at last, she believed, in a pristine landscape where natives had lived in innocence for hundreds of years, she found the place where she could fulfill her destiny.

With the help of Antonio Lujan, a Tiwa with whom she fell in love, she purchased property in Taos and began building a home. She and Tony divorced their respective spouses and married in 1923, at which time Mabel became Mabel Dodge Luhan (spelling her last name with an "h" rather than a "j" so it would be pronounced correctly). Convinced that Taos held answers for others, too—as a place where fugitives from modern civilization could connect with nature and experience the deep rhythms of life, if only for a time—she created an estate large enough to be shared. Using local builders supervised by Tony and beginning with an old adobe house that she remodeled and expanded, Mabel created Los Gallos, a compound that eventually included a Big House with seventeen rooms, a gatehouse for her staff of servants, five guest houses, and assorted stables and barns, all in the vernacular Pueblo style. She then opened her doors to selected friends, artists, and intellectuals who might benefit from the healing power of the southwest—Ansel Adams, Mary Austin, Willa Cather, Martha Graham, Carl Jung, Georgia O'Keeffe, Edward Weston, and Thornton Wilder, among them.

One of the first major figures to visit her was D. H. Lawrence, who was induced by Mabel to come to Taos in 1922. "I willed him to come," says Mabel in an account written later. "Before I went to sleep at night, I drew myself all in to the core of my being where there is a live, plangent force lying passive—waiting for direction. Becoming entirely that, moving with it, speaking with it, I leaped through space, joining myself to the central core of Lawrence" and "I became that action that brought him across the sea." The silent incantation,

"'Come Lawrence! Come to Taos!' became, in me," she says, "Lawrence in Taos. This is not prayer, but command."

Lawrence and his wife Frieda surrendered to Mabel and dutifully arrived at Los Gallos, but Lawrence was not altogether pleased with Mabel. In a December 5, 1922 letter to his mother-in-law, Lawrence describes Mabel as

a little famous in New York and little loved, very intelligent as a woman, another "culture carrier," likes to play the patroness, hates the white world and loves the Indian out of hate, is very "generous," wants to be "good" and is very wicked, has a terrible will-to-power, you know—she wants to be a witch and at the same time a Mary of Bethany at Jesus's feet—a big, white crow, a cooing raven of ill omen, a little buffalo.

Mabel did what she could to keep Lawrence in Taos, even giving him a ranch where he and Frieda and their friend Dorothy Brett could live on their own, but he eventually returned to Europe and left unfinished the work Mabel had planned for him, which was to be the artistic medium through which the secrets of the southwest would be revealed to the larger world. Already looking for someone to replace Lawrence when he died in March 1930, Mabel was in Carmel, with her sights set on Jeffers.

Jeffers himself was out of Mabel's reach—he had no interest in anything but his own work and family—but Una was not, and Mabel quickly cultivated an intimate friendship with her. Mabel's plan, as Spud Johnson openly describes it in an article titled "She Did It" published in the *Carmelite*

May 29, 1930, was to move in close to the Jeffers family, invite Garth and Donnan to New Mexico for the summer, and then, after arrangements were made and the twins were suitably excited, withdraw the invitation unless Robinson and Una came with them. Though her enticements were at first met with "the blank wall of the Jeffers' resolution (made when they returned from their strenuous European venture) not to stir again for years," by the beginning of June the Jeffers family was on the road to Taos for a month's vacation.

When they arrived, they were treated as honored guests. Garth and Donnan were given overalls, sombreros, and bandanas; Una wore a Navajo jacket. Horseback riding, ranch activities, swimming, trips to nearby Taos Pueblo, and journeys into the mountains filled each day. There were fiestas to attend, daily banquets to enjoy, and opportunities to observe native dancers and special ceremonies. Jeffers appreciated the chance to see the countryside, but it did not inspire him the way Luhan hoped it would. While he was in Taos or after he returned to Carmel, he wrote exactly one poem about his experience, "New Mexican Mountain." The poem recounts Jeffers' attendance at a corn dance performed by "shame-faced young men" for paying Americans. Rather than celebrating the vitality of the people and the place, the poem expresses Jeffers' perception of cultural malaise. The empty tourists, "anxious to be human again," suck the life out of the natives. "Only the drum is confident," Jeffers says; only the drum, he himself, and the ancient mountain know that "civilization is a transient sickness" and that both the dancers and those who watch them are lost.

"New Mexican Mountain" appeared in the September 5, 1931 issue of the *Saturday Review of Literature*. Had Luhan read the poem, perhaps she would not have bothered to publish *Lorenzo in Taos*, which was released early in 1932. In this book, composed as a long letter to Jeffers, Luhan describes her successful efforts to lure Lawrence to Taos, his adventures and her battles with him there, and his inability or unwillingness to complete the task she set for him. "Well, Jeffers," Luhan says near the end of her narrative, "that is all I have to tell you about Lawrence in Taos. I called him there, but he did not do what I called him to do. He did another thing. Perhaps you are the one who will, after all, do what I wanted him to do: give a voice to this speechless land."

It did not happen. In the first half of the decade, despite month-long visits to Taos in 1930, 1933, 1934, and 1935, Jeffers never wrote a word about the southwest, except for the poem already mentioned. During this time, Mabel's son John brought his family to Carmel and drew close to Robinson and Una; Mabel herself visited Carmel frequently, spending over four months there in 1933; but even the tightening bonds of family friendship and the pressure of Mabel's continuing campaign could not induce Jeffers to write about New Mexico. Instead, after each vacation there, he set the experience aside and returned with single-minded devotion to his own poetic concerns.

Jeffers published four books during this period: *Descent to the Dead: Poems Written in Ireland and Great Britain* (1931), *Thurso's Landing and Other Poems* (1932), *Give Your Heart to the Hawks and Other Poems* (1933), and *Solstice and Other Poems* (1935). An expanded, Modern Library edition of *Roan Stallion, Tamar and Other Poems* also came out in 1935.

Descent to the Dead (1931) contains sixteen poems written by Jeffers during his 1929 trip to the British Isles (which indicates a willingness to write about contemporary places other than the Big Sur if inspired to do so). With permission from Horace Liveright, Jeffers' publisher, the finely bound book was released by Random House in a limited edition of 500 copies. Demand was so great that the edition sold out prior to printing. In such poems as "Shane O'Neill's Cairn," "Ossian's Grave," "In the Hill at Newgrange," and "Iona: The Graves of the Kings," Jeffers offers an extended meditation on mortality, the burden of history, and the primacy of the nether world. In "Ghosts in England," Jeffers describes spirits seen throughout the country, unconcerned about signs of collapse: "They seemed merry, and to feel / No pity for the great pillar of empire settling to a fall, the pride and the power slowly dissolving."

The title poem of *Thurso's Landing and Other Poems* (1932) tells the story of Reave Thurso, a strong-willed man living in the Big Sur with his frustrated wife, stern mother, and lame, weak-minded brother. Their cabin in Mill Creek Canyon is about all they have left of a once-successful lime-kiln and lumber mill operation. Reave's father owned the business, and when it failed, he killed himself. A rusting skip, once used to transport lime, still hangs in the canyon, suspended from a long steel cable and serving as a daily reminder of failure and loss. After Reave's wife Helen runs away with a road construction worker, and after Reave tracks her for a year and brings her home, he decides to cut the cable down. When he attempts to do so, the heavy cable unravels at an unexpected moment and strikes his back, flaying his skin and leaving him paralyzed from the waist down. Helen, having already resigned herself to her fate—which is to stay with Reave—turns to him with compassion after the accident. Unable to endure his suffering, she kills him and then kills herself. Reave's brother, broken by the family's history of defeat, had already committed suicide. In the end, Reave's stalwart mother is left alone. Along with the long title poem, *Thurso's Landing* contains a briefer narrative titled *Margrave* and nine short lyrics. Among the lyrics, "The Place for No Story" and "Fire on the Hills" extol the fierce beauty of the Big Sur coast.

Thurso's Landing was released March 24, 1932. Ten days later, on April 4, *Time* magazine featured a striking cover photograph of Jeffers by Edward Weston. "Such is the theme, such the characters of a new poem by Robinson Jeffers," says an accompanying review essay, "whom a considerable public now considers the most impressive poet the U.S. has yet produced." In the same month, *Vanity Fair* published a photograph of Jeffers and his sons. "In the eyes of many," the caption reports, "Robinson Jeffers is America's greatest poet."

Thurso's Landing was the last book by Jeffers published by Liveright. Poor investments by the firm's owner, along with losses incurred during the Depression, led to the firm's demise. In the midst of the collapse, nearly every major publisher in America approached Jeffers with an offer of a long-term contract. According to Bennett Cerf in *At*

Random, "it was obvious there was going to be a raid on what few important authors" the company had left. "Everybody was making offers for Eugene O'Neill, and also for one of the leading American poets on the Liveright list, Robinson Jeffers." Those were "the two I wanted most," said Cerf, and after making special trips to Sea Island, Georgia to see O'Neill and to Carmel to talk with Jeffers, he signed both of them. Even though Jeffers' books were not best sellers like O'Neill's, they sold well for poetry and "there was great prestige in publishing him." Understandably proud of his accomplishment, Cerf released the following statement in mid-1933: "Random House is pleased to announce that it has become the exclusive publisher in America of the books of Eugene O'Neill and Robinson Jeffers."

Give Your Heart to the Hawks and Other Poems, Jeffers' first major book with Random House, appeared in September 1933. Roosevelt was in his first term as president at this time. While he and his aides were taking aggressive steps to end the Depression, millions of people were still out of work, thousands of banks were failing, business assets were in decline, and a drought was ruining farmlands. Despite these conditions, and despite the severity of Jeffers' worldview, a deluxe limited edition of 500 copies of *Give Your Heart to the Hawks* and a regular trade edition of 3,000 copies both sold out immediately, and the book was reprinted in October.

The title poem of *Give Your Heart to the Hawks* recounts another domestic tragedy. Fayne Fraser, a beautiful young woman with flaming red hair, is married to Lance Fraser, a muscular rancher. During a bonfire picnic on the beach with Lance's brother Michael, other friends, and their dates, Lance's mind slowly darkens from the effects of whiskey, a brooding disposition, and jealousy. When, after a brief altercation with Fayne, he finds her beneath a cliff with Michael, he strikes his brother with a steel bolt found in a piece of driftwood, killing him instantly. Remorse is followed by an urge to confess, but Fayne's quick-thinking cover-up leads everyone to believe that Michael fell from the cliff and struck his head on a rock, though suspicions among the friends remain. Returning home, where Lance and Fayne live with Lance's parents (and where Michael had lived as well), Lance tries to continue life as if everything were normal. Guilt overwhelms him, however, and he becomes increasingly distracted, self-absorbed, and brutal. Elements from Greek mythology, such as the vengeance of the Furies and the madness of Ajax (when the stricken hero attacks a herd of oxen), deepen the story, as do motifs from the Bible, such as Cain's murder of his brother Abel. In the end, Lance commits suicide, and Fayne, pregnant and unscathed, continues on.

In addition to the long title poem, all the poems previously published in *Descent to the Dead*, and six short lyrics, *Give Your Heart to the Hawks* contains two other works that deserve mention, both over twenty pages in length. A verse drama, *At the Fall of an Age*, concludes the book. Inspired by a passage in *Descriptions of Greece* by Pausanias (Book III, Chapter 19), the drama recounts Helen's arrival at Rhodes, where she hopes to find sanctuary with an old friend, Polyxo. The Trojan War has long since ended, Menelaus is dead, and Helen, hated everywhere, has no home. Polyxo hates her, too, Helen soon

11 Robinson Jeffers, 1933

discovers, primarily because Polyxo's husband was among the thousands of men who died for her. Rather than accepting her as a guest, Polyxo calls for a rope, strips Helen, and hangs her. Before Helen dies and before Polyxo herself is killed by a local fisherman, Polyxo learns that the men who brought Helen to Rhodes on a black ship are actually dead Myrmidons, raised from the grave by the will of Achilles. The dead hero had come back to life in order to possess Helen; now, having done so, he was on his way to White Island, one of the Islands of the Blessed, henceforth his eternal home. After Helen's death on Rhodes, Pausanias reports, she was worshipped there as "Helen Dendritis"—"Helen of the Trees."

By itself, *At the Fall of an Age* might seem to be a literary diversion, prompted by an evening reading classics by the fire. Seen in connection with *Resurrection*, the other twenty-page poem in *Give Your Heart to the Hawks*, it is clearly much more than that. *Resurrection*, appearing just before *At the Fall of an Age*, also involves a soldier who, for the love of a woman, returns from the dead. In this case, the woman is named Hildis and the soldier Carson. Hildis lives in a cabin in the Big Sur with her husband George Ramsay and two children. One night, as she drifts into sleep, she dreams of a dog scrambling up from a burrow, all covered with earth. A few moments later, when her husband comes to bed and mechanically makes love to her, she thinks, with a wandering mind, of people rising from their graves. A few weeks after that, when an earthquake lifts the mountain, she imagines a being with bloody shoulders struggling to break free. Finally, when mushrooms sprout in a moist crack in the earth, they look to Hildis like the fingers of dead people reaching toward the light. Each experience prefigures the actual arrival of Carson, the father of her first child, who knocks at the cabin door on a rainy night. He had been killed in France during World War I. Rather than lying in his grave in peace, he dreamed of Hildis—enough so that his spirit, unwilling to let go, eventually refleshed itself, rose up, and found its way to her door. The poem ends with Hildis choosing to go with Carson; they leave the cabin together and disappear into the darkness.

Given Jeffers' mythopoetic imagination, which enabled him to see the world with both solar and lunar vision (with, that is, the clear light of reason and the intuitive wisdom of dream), *Resurrection* and *At the Fall of an Age* are more than simple ghost stories. Their themes—the horror of war, the return of soldiers from the dead, the sacrifice of beauty, the need for satisfaction and revenge—serve as premonitions. At a time when most of his contemporaries in America were thinking about the depressed economy and, if politically inclined, the value or threat of communism, fears of a looming war had not yet taken hold. Jeffers, however, could feel the tremors.

Early in 1933, as Jeffers was putting the finishing touches on *Give Your Heart to the Hawks*, with *Resurrection* and *At the Fall of an Age* already written, Adolf Hitler completed his rise to power. In January, Hitler became chancellor of Germany. In February, after the Reichstag fire, his coalition government suspended civil liberties. In March, following the Nazi victory in national elections, Hitler assumed the role of dictator. Also in March, he opened his first prison camp, at Dachau. In April, Hitler ordered a boycott of Jewish businesses and created the Gestapo. In the following months, trade unions were banned, books were burned, eugenic sterilization was legalized, and all non-Nazi political parties were forbidden. Accordingly, by the time *Give Your Heart to the Hawks* came out in September, Hitler's long-simmering rage over Germany's defeat in World War I and his glorious dreams for Germany's future were beginning to threaten the world.

Solstice and Other Poems (1935) is more deliberately ominous. Poems in the book refer both to the natural cycle of life and death on Earth and the rise and fall of nations. In "Rearmament," for instance, Jeffers compares "frost in November" to the "grand and fatal movements toward death" observed in mass cultures. In "Flight of Swans," Orion's appearance in the midnight sky of winter provides the backdrop for the image of a rocket, symbolizing civilization, wavering at its zenith and just about to fall. In *Solstice*, the mid-length narrative that provides the title for the book, the collapse of human institutions is described in terms of conflict between two people. The story concerns Madrone Bothwell, a recently divorced woman. At the time of the winter solstice, just before Christmas, Madrone learns that her husband Andrew has sold their home in the Big Sur, which she must vacate; furthermore, he has won custody of their two children. When he arrives with an attorney and two other men to take the children away, she kills the boy and girl—and then flees with their bodies to the snow-covered mountains, never to be seen again.

Jeffers probably had the Greek myth of Medea in mind when he composed *Solstice*, but another source might have been a medieval epic, the *Völsung Saga*, wherein Gudrun kills her children to spite her husband Atli (Attila the Hun). The *Völsung Saga* is a likely influence because Jeffers turned to it for *At the Birth of an Age*, the first poem in *Solstice* and companion to *At the Fall of an Age*, the last poem in *Give Your Heart to the Hawks*.

As Jeffers tells the story (diverging significantly from the Icelandic original), three brothers—Gunnar, Hoegni, and Carling—are on their way to see their estranged sister Gudrun at her behest. A few years prior to this meeting, Gunnar and Hoegni murdered Gudrun's husband Sigurd. Gudrun is now the wife of Attila, the most powerful warlord in northern and central Europe, and the brothers are unsure of her intentions. Does she want peace or does she want to kill them? As it turns out, she wants both. After asking Attila to execute Gunnar and Hoegni, she changes her mind, but by this time the brothers are already imprisoned. In an effort to free them, Carling mounts a raid in which all three brothers die. Gudrun then plunges a dagger into her own heart.

The action of Jeffers' verse drama takes place on the eve of one of Western Civilization's most decisive battles. In 451 CE, a coalition of forces led by the Christian Visigoth king, Theodoric, and the Roman commander-in-chief, Aetius, met the army of Attila on a field near Paris, between the Seine and the Marne. Attila, from his base above the Danube, had already sacked Cologne, Mainz, Strasbourg, Trier, and many other cities in a brutal campaign to conquer all of Europe. Theodoric (who died in the battle) and Aetius defeated Attila, and, from then on, the fearsome Huns declined in power.

For Jeffers, as he says in a prose preface to the poem, the Christian/Roman victory at Châlons-sur-Marne marked the beginning of a new age in Western Civilization—the Christian Age: "the greatest, but also the most bewildered and self-contradictory, the least integrated, in some phases the most ignoble, that has ever existed." Now, after fifteen hundred years, with spring, summer, and autumn behind it, the culture that came out of the Dark Ages, that "drew taut the frail arches of Gothic cathedrals" and created the modern world, had finally reached winter. "I believe," Jeffers says, finding another way to describe the turning point, "that we live about the summit of the wave of this age, and hence can see it more objectively, looking down toward the troughs on both sides."

Given the logic of *Solstice* as a whole, where life and death are linked on an ever-turning wheel, a view of the past is also a view of the future. Accordingly, Jeffers' story about the tense moments just before a major battle in 451 CE was also a story about 1935—where Attila stands for Hitler, Hun means "German soldier" (a conventional meaning of the term during and after World War I), and an invasion of Gaul threatens all of Europe. Many readers no doubt missed the message, frightened into blindness by the prospect of another war, but Jeffers' warning was plain to see.

Along with its burden of prophecy, *At the Birth of an Age* also carries another heavy weight: a vision of God, one of the most remarkable in all of American literature. A culminating theophany, similar to Krishna's in the *Bhagavad-Gita* or Yahweh's in the Book of Job, is preceded by references to Prometheus, Wotan, and Christ, all of whom are "rough deific sketches," in the words of Walt Whitman, of the one true God. An image of Prometheus, chained to a rock on

Mt. Elboros and bleeding from his side, is painted on a wall of the ruined Roman villa where the action of *At the Birth of an Age* takes place. As the drama unfolds, the image prompts comparisons to Wotan, the god of Gudrun and her brothers, who hanged himself on the World Tree, and to Christ, the god of the Bishop of Troyes and his fellow Christians, who died on the Cross. All three self-sacrificing gods, along with similar deities in other cultures, derive from and refer to the one, all-encompassing God of the universe—the Hanged God, as Jeffers identifies him here, who, conscious and alone, endures pain for the sake of self-knowledge.

First experienced by Jeffers during his awakening in 1919, central to his pantheistic vision thereafter, and described in luminous passages of verse in each successive book, the self-tormenting deity appears at the end of *At the Birth of an Age* and speaks to himself for all to hear. "Pain and their endless cries," the Hanged God says in response to the sound of suffering he hears—

> How they cry to me: but they are I: let them ask
> themselves.
> I am they, and there is nothing beside. I am alone and time passes, time
> also is in me, the long
> Beat of this unquiet heart, the quick drip of this blood, the whirl and
> returning waves of these stars,
> The course of this thought.
> . . . I am all, the emptiness and all, the shining and the
> night.
> All alone, I alone.

Conscious of the cosmos as a whole in the way all embodied
beings are conscious, God—who "has no righteousness, /
No mercy, no love"—lives for experience.

          If I were quiet and emptied myself of pain,
    breaking these bonds,
Healing these wounds: without strain there is nothing. Without
    pressure, without conditions, without pain,
Is peace; that's nothing, not-being; the pure night, the perfect freedom,
    the black crystal. I have chosen
Being; therefore wounds, bonds, limits and pain; the crowded mind
    and the anguished nerves, experience and ecstasy.

Whatever electron or atom or flesh or star or universe cries to me,
Or endures in shut silence: it is my cry, my silence; I am the nerve, I am
    the agony,
I am the endurance. I torture myself
To discover myself; trying with a little or extreme experiment each
    nerve and fibril, all forms
Of being, of life, of cold substance; all motions and netted
    complications of event,
All poisons of desire, love, hatred, joy, partial peace, partial vision.
    Discovery is deep and endless,
Each moment of being is new: therefore I still refrain my burning
    thirst from the crystal-black
Water of an end.

1935–1940

The first issue of *Life* magazine, as published by Henry Luce, appeared November 23, 1936. The cover featured a photograph by Margaret Bourke-White of Fort Peck Dam, then under construction in northeastern Montana. Two men in the photograph stand before the massive steel and concrete floodgates designed to manage the flow of the Missouri River. With America still fighting the Great Depression, the photograph offered a reassuring message of human mastery.

A motto for the 1930s might well have been "Take Control." Frightened by uncertainty and committed to progress, Americans placed their hopes in science, engineering, technology, and management—all in the service of government. Franklin Delano Roosevelt began his first term in office by declaring "the only thing we have to fear is fear itself." When campaigning for a second term, which he won by a landslide three weeks before the first issue of *Life* came out, his rallying cry was "we have not yet begun to fight." The New Deal agencies he created—such as the Farm Security Administration, Federal Deposit Insurance Corporation, Public Works Administration, Security and Exchange Commission, Social Security Administration, Tennessee Valley Authority, Works Progress Administration, and United States Housing Authority—extended the supervisory reach of the federal government into virtually every area of American life.

Some projects sponsored by the government, like the one at Fort Peck, met the immediate needs of thousands of men and women who otherwise would have been unemployed.

They also provided long-term benefits, such as flood control, an improved water supply, new recreational opportunities, and the generation of hydroelectric power. Similar projects elsewhere—such as the Shasta Dam in California, the Grand Coulee and Bonneville Dams in Washington and Oregon, and the Norris, Wheeler, and Pickwick Landing Dams in Tennessee—harnessed the power of the Sacramento, Columbia, Clinch, and Tennessee Rivers. The massive Hoover Dam on the border between Nevada and Arizona, built by 21,000 workers between 1931 and 1936, collared the mighty Colorado River and provided a dependable source of water and electricity to thirsty Los Angeles and other southwestern cities.

In addition to the dams (and the vast reservoirs behind them) that radically altered the physical landscape of America, 78,000 large and small bridges were built by government workers throughout the country. Among them were such engineering masterpieces as the Henry Hudson and Triborough Bridges in New York and the Bay and Golden Gate Bridges in California, all of which opened to traffic between 1936 and 1938. On either side of the bridges, roads were laid down, hundreds of thousands of miles of them—crossing plains, cutting through forests, tunneling through mountains, and joining rural and urban areas together in one vast concrete thoroughfare.

Prior to the 1930s, the Big Sur was impassable along the coast. The roundabout route between Carmel and San Simeon (90 miles south) was inland. When the Bixby Creek Bridge—an extraordinary structure composed of a single, towering concrete arch—was completed in 1932, and when additional bridges were erected over four other nearby canyons, the key components for a more direct route were in place. Five more years passed before the Carmel–San Simeon portion of Highway 1 was finished. After a dedication ceremony held June 27, 1937, the central coast of California was officially opened to throughway traffic. Jeffers expressed his feelings about the project in a poem titled "The Coast-Road." A horseman in the poem, looking down from a mountain, shakes his fist at "the bridge-builders, men, trucks, the power-shovels" before turning to ride higher. "I too / Believe," Jeffers says, "that the life of men who ride horses, herders of cattle on the mountain pasture, plowers of remote / Rock-narrowed farms in poverty and freedom, is a good life." He then adds:

> At the far end of those loops of road
> Is what will come and destroy it, a rich and vulgar and bewildered
>   civilization dying at the core,
> A world that is feverishly preparing new wars, peculiarly vicious ones,
>   and heavier tyrannies, a strangely
> Missionary world, road-builder, wind-rider, educator, printer and
>   picture-maker and broad-caster,
> So eager, like an old drunken whore, pathetically eager to impose the
>   seduction of her fled charms
> On all that through ignorance or isolation might have escaped them.

While Robinson and Una were still lighting their home with oil lamps and heating it with firewood, the rest of the country was hurrying to electrify and modernize. People driving north or south on Highway 1 between Los Angeles and San Francisco now came within a mile or so of Tor House. The cars they were driving, like the DeSoto Airstream or the Chrysler Airflow, were designed with aerodynamic principles in mind, replete with decorative speed lines. The sleek, Streamline style could be found on the Pioneer Zephyr, a locomotive also called the Silver Streak that, with its matching cars, skimmed the rails twice as fast as other trains, and on the new Douglas DC-3, an aircraft sheathed in stainless steel that revolutionized transcontinental air travel. Radios, clocks, lamps, and other household goods reiterated the Streamline style and thus reaffirmed notions of fast, forward momentum and "progress." During the Machine Age, as cultural historians call this period in American history, signs of modern industry and, thus, human dominion, were everywhere.

In painting, photography, and sculpture, works depicting factories, large construction projects, machines, and machine parts proliferated. Representative examples, with titles like *Manhattan Bridge: Looking Up* and *Lathe, Akeley Machine Shop*, were created by Berenice Abbott, Paul Strand, Margaret Bourke-White, and many other artists. An exhibit at New York's Museum of Modern Art in 1934 reinforced the notion that art and industry were related. Titled Machine Art, the exhibit featured over 400 commercially available items—everything from lamps and chairs to an outboard motor and dental instruments—all designed with both aesthetic and utilitarian principles in mind.

In architecture, modern design was often as close as the nearest service station. The plain rectangular buildings erected by Standard Oil, for instance, were neat, clean, and efficient-looking. With their flat roofs and grid-like glass walls, they epitomized the Bauhaus-inspired International Style. The "form follows function" principle also influenced the design of factories, schools, and office buildings. Housing, too, especially large apartment projects, expressed Le Corbusier's belief that "a house is a machine for living in."

Even poetry was affected by these convictions. As William Carlos Williams later said in his introduction to *The Wedge*, "A poem is a small (or large) machine made of words." One might also argue that literary criticism—specifically, the New Criticism that flourished in the 1930s and beyond—was shaped by the Machine Age point of view. Poems were regarded as discrete artifacts, ultimately disconnected from their creators and amenable to mechanical analysis. To understand how a poem works, preferably a short poem, one simply dismantles it and studies its component parts.

Jeffers was not opposed to science, technology, and human progress in principle. Throughout his life, certainly from the time of his medical studies on, he stayed abreast of new discoveries in astronomy, biology, geography, physics, and other fields, and he incorporated current discoveries into his work. Nevertheless, he was mindful of the fact that scientific research and technological invention are human enterprises, which means their motives, means, and ends are compromised by self-centeredness.

The title poem of *Such Counsels You Gave to Me and Other Poems*, published by Jeffers in late September 1937, tells the story of Howard Howren, a student at the University of

California, Berkeley, who returns to his parents' ranch in the Big Sur with a shattered mind. Unable to support himself and continue his studies in biochemistry (specifically, the evolution of pre-cellular life), he has resolved to beg his father, called Howren in the poem, for financial help. If his brutish father refuses, as expected, he plans to kill himself with cyanide stolen from the university laboratory. Howard's mother Barbara, also mentally unstable, sides with her son. When Howard's father does, in fact, refuse to help him—wanting Howard to work on the ranch rather than go to school—his mother, filled with years of repressed bitterness and having discovered the vial of poison in her son's pocket, suggests murder. Soon after, on a night when Howren returns home drunk, he shares a few nightcaps with his wife and son. Two last glasses of liquor are poured and, urged on by his mother, Howard adds the poison to one of them. Not knowing for sure which is which, he picks a glass and downs it, watching as his father does the same. Within seconds, the rancher dies, thrashing wildly and gasping for air.

Howard is a scientist and thus, supposedly, a rational human being dedicated to the selfless pursuit of truth. As aspects of Howard's personality become clear, however, various neuroses are revealed, including a panoply of Oedipal conflicts. At the base of his thirst for knowledge is a high school lesson learned from Mendel: blue-eyed parents cannot produce a dark-eyed child. Since Howard's parents were blue-eyed, and since the eyes of Howard's younger sister, France, were brown, it followed that Howard's mother had committed adultery. The sublimated distress engendered by this discovery, kept secret through the years, led to his "feverish interest in all the sciences of life."

In the aftermath of the murder, as Howard and his mother confront what they have done, long-repressed tensions seep through the cracks of their psyches. Having already committed patricide, one of humankind's worst imaginable crimes, Howard is unable to restrain another compulsion. Touching his mother lightly on the face, he says, "'I have something / Strange to ask you. Will you show me your breasts?'" His mother complies, and offers all of herself to her son, but desire in Howard soon turns to revulsion. As he reaches out to help her draw her dress back over her shoulders, her mind breaks into pieces and her body is convulsed with screams.

The scene reminds one of Louis-Ernest Barrias' famous statue, *Nature Unveiling Herself Before Science* (1899). Where, however, Barrias imagines a demure maiden eager to share her naked beauty with an admiring suitor (leaving the Oedipal conflicts latent, since it is a youthful Mother Nature who subjects herself to the viewer's gaze), Jeffers sees outright depravity and obsession. The probing eyes of science, he implies, are not innocent. Nor, to carry the thought further, are the hands of technology pure.

A passing reference in *Such Counsels You Gave to Me* makes Jeffers' point. Just after Howard pours the poison into the whiskey, he notes the strangeness of the situation. "Nothing like this could be," he says to himself, with his heart pounding, and then aloud: "'but as real as Europe's / Rearmament race . . . or Dirac's equations: / Nothing is real this year.'" Paul Dirac's discovery, for which he was awarded the Nobel Prize in 1933, involved a relativistic wave equation for the electron. As a major contribution to quantum physics, the discovery transformed science's understanding of subatomic matter. In little more than a decade, Dirac's equations, along with those of other brilliant theorists, were used by members of Roosevelt's Manhattan Project, another government enterprise with roots in the New Deal, to create "Little Boy" and "Fat Man," the atomic bombs exploded over Hiroshima and Nagasaki. Tens of thousands of men, women, and children, along with untold numbers of other living beings, lost their lives in the 7,000-degree firestorms and 600 mph winds.

There are no saviors in Jeffers' world. For thousands of years, people depended on faith for answers to life's basic questions; for hundreds of years, at least since the Scientific Revolution, the intelligentsia depended on reason. For Jeffers, both faith and reason, religion and science, are flawed. In a poem titled "Theory of Truth," written at the same time as *Such Counsels You Gave to Me* but too late for inclusion in the book, Jeffers refers to Lao-tze, the Buddha, and Jesus. "Only tormented persons want truth," he says of them, adding that each was driven by a "private agony" to probe the unknown. Consequently, the answers they found, eventually codified in faith, have "aching strands of insanity in them." Jesus, for instance, solved the problem of his illegitimate birth by saying he was the Son of God—and people who follow him share the same delusion. The torment seen in Lao-tze, the Buddha, and Jesus is characteristic of humans generally. It shows up in religious visionaries like Rev. Barclay in *The Women at Point Sur* and scientists like Howard Howren in *Such Counsels You Gave to Me*, both of whom are cut from the same cloth. In the real world, it also appears in charismatic heads of state, whose goal is not truth but power—as a close look at the inner lives of Franco, Hirohito, Hitler, Mussolini, Stalin, and other leaders of the time, including Roosevelt, would reveal.

Informed by these convictions, the shorter poems in *Such Counsels You Gave to Me* are generally elegiac in tone, even as they offer dire warnings: "We have geared the machines and locked all together into interdependence; we have built the great cities; now / There is no escape" ("The Purse-Seine"); "I see far fires and dim degradation / Under the war-planes and neither Christ nor Lenin will save you" ("Air-Raid Rehearsals"); "The age weakens and settles home toward old ways. / An age of renascent faith: Christ said, Marx wrote, Hitler says, / And though it seems absurd we believe" ("Thebaid"); "Change and the world, we think, are racing to a fall, / Open-eyed and helpless, in every news-cast that is the news" ("Hope Is Not for the Wise"); "the present time is not pastoral, but founded / On violence, pointed for more massive violence" ("Self-Criticism in February"); "The age darkens, Europe mixes her cups of death, all the little Caesars fidget on their thrones" ("Hellenistics"). "Cruelty and filth and superstition"—the willingness to harm others, pollute the world, and believe anything—are at the root of human problems, Jeffers declares in the last named poem, and all three are destined to persist.

In addition to warnings, several poems offer advice on how to maintain integrity and live authentically. An essential step in this endeavor, as Jeffers says in "The Wind-Struck

Music," "Nova," "Oh, Lovely Rock," "The Beaks of Eagles," and "Night Without Sleep," is to open one's heart and mind to the larger, natural world outside human civilization. To think in terms of geological and astronomical time, to see "the enormous invulnerable beauty" of the universe in its entirety and the "perfect loveliness" of its infinitely varied parts—on Earth, a water-ouzel perched on a stone, a snake with two delicate scarlet lines running down its back, the hoof-prints of deer in the dust; in the heavens, the spectacle of an exploding star—is to escape the stifling grasp of human enterprise and to experience what, for Jeffers, is the sum and substance of enlightenment. In "The Answer," he states his position clearly:

Then what is the answer?—Not to be deluded by dreams.
To know that great civilizations have broken down into violence, and
    their tyrants come, many times before.
When open violence appears, to avoid it with honor or choose the
    least ugly faction; these evils are essential.
To keep one's own integrity, be merciful and uncorrupted and not wish
    for evil; and not be duped
By dreams of universal justice or happiness. These dreams will not be
    fulfilled.
To know this, and know that however ugly the parts appear the whole
    remains beautiful. A severed hand
Is an ugly thing, and man dissevered from the earth and stars and his
    history . . . for contemplation or in fact . . .
Often appears atrociously ugly. Integrity is wholeness, the greatest
    beauty is

Organic wholeness, the wholeness of life and things, the divine beauty
   of the universe. Love that, not man
Apart from that, or else you will share man's pitiful confusions, or
   drown in despair when his days darken.

Jeffers himself lived according to these principles, much to the chagrin of friends, critics, and readers who were more committed to social and political activism. Except for contributing a manuscript to an auction organized by Langston Hughes as a fund-raising event for the defense of the Scottsboro Boys in 1935, Jeffers usually stayed out of public affairs. He declined, for instance, to sign on as a sponsor or even attend the Western Writers' Congress in San Francisco in November 1936, a gathering inspired by the communist-backed American Writers' Congress held in New York over a year before. The Western Congress was dedicated to the memory of political journalist Lincoln Steffens, who died in August; Ella Winter, Sara Bard Field, and Charles Erskine Scott Wood played key roles. The object of the event was to create a community among working writers, to explore ways they could help each other achieve common goals, and to speak out against fascism—none of which, as a collective enterprise, appealed to Jeffers. As he said in his August 1936 letter of regret, "It seems to me quite useless, for writers cannot be organized—except newspaper or film writers—and ought to associate with any or all classes in the community rather than with each other; and if they wish to express opinions they can write them. And I do not think that culture can be maintained or handed down through conventions and committees."

Jeffers also turned down Van Wyck Brooks' invitation to add his name to a statement that denounced atrocities committed by Nationalists in the Spanish Civil War. The statement, signed by nearly a hundred writers (including Sherwood Anderson, William Faulkner, Langston Hughes, Sinclair Lewis, Edgar Lee Masters, Carl Sandburg, Thornton Wilder, and William Carlos Williams), was printed in the March 1, 1937 edition of the *New York Times*. In his letter to Brooks, Jeffers says "I would sign this statement if it protested the atrocities committed on both sides," but "I am not willing to go on record in favor of either side." A year later, Jeffers responded to a similar appeal the same way. A point-blank question from the president of the League of American Writers—"Are you for, or are you against Franco and fascism? Are you for, or are you against the legal government and the people of Republican Spain?"—elicited over 400 responses, published as *Writers Take Sides* in May 1938. All but eight respondents (98 percent) supported the Loyalists and denounced Franco. Jeffers' response was nonpartisan. "You ask what I am for and what against in Spain," he answers. "I would give my right hand, of course, to prevent the agony; I would not give a flick of my little finger to help either side win." Throughout the volatile 1930s, Jeffers remained true to his ideals, knowing how unpopular that would make him. As he states in "The Great Sunset," "'To be truth-bound, the neutral / Detested by all the dreaming factions, is my errand here.'"

Neutrality increased rather than diminished Jeffers' sympathetic reaction to the world. He saw suffering on both sides of a conflict—and everywhere he looked. In "Memoir," yet another signal poem in *Such Counsels You Gave to Me*, he refers to sick monkeys, dying rats, "throat-bandaged dogs cowering in cages, still obsessed with the pitiful / Love that dogs feel, longing to lick the hand of their devil," and, by extension, all laboratory animals who, as subjects of scientific experiments, are "sacrificed / To human inquisitiveness, pedantry and vanity." He also refers to ranch hands in the Big Sur driving frightened steers into frames that hold them for de-horning. As one man removes the horns by crushing them with a tool that looks like pruning shears, another cakes "the blood-fountains with burning alum."

Scientists and ranch hands, Jeffers says, are oblivious to the pain they cause. Such men, like most other people, "are fit for life," and they "rarely feel pain outside their own skins"—while he himself, like a dowser, goes "here and there / With skinless pity for the dipping hazel-fork." Standing amidst lupine and sage after a bracing rain, Jeffers knows he need not think of the laboratories and cattle-pens; he need not think of the "million persons" presently "dying of hunger in the provinces of China," or of "the Russian labor-camps, the German / Prison-camps," or any of the countless other pulsing centers of torment "That make the earth shine like a star with cruelty for light"; he need not think "of the probable wars, tyranny and pain / Made world-wide"; and finally, he need not "know that this is our world, where only fool or drunkard makes happy songs"— but he could not do otherwise.

Jeffers, like planet Earth, had a molten interior around which a thick mantle of stone had formed. The surface of his psyche, exposed to all sensation, was subject to tectonic strain—as Una well knew. In a May 1934 letter to Phoebe Barkan, Una writes,

Life has been going smoothly here.—me sitting on the lid! We have gone off for one whole day by ourselves in the hills every week and walked for two hours late afternoons almost every day & Robin has been content. *No*, there hasn't been any *real* intention of deserting Carmel—its only I have said now and again—"If I can't manage to give Robin an illusion of a wilder, more rural home, we'll have to go elsewhere." Somehow I've managed to give that illusion.

By 1937, the year Jeffers turned fifty, signs of stress were even more pronounced—which is one of the reasons Una proposed another trip to the British Isles.

Robinson, Una, and their sons left home in June. They drove their car across the country, loaded it on a ship, and sailed for Ireland. After landing in Cobh, in County Cork on the southern coast, they made their way north, visiting a number of sites along the way, including St. Patrick's Mountain, George Moore's burial place, Yeats' tower, Galway, the Aran Islands, and Connemara. In County Donegal, on the remote north coast, they took rooms in Lac-na-Lore, a small inn near Ballymore. With that as their base for more than a month, they toured the surrounding countryside, stopped to visit Glenveagh Castle, climbed Errigal and Muckish Mountains, and explored places like the Bloody Foreland, the Poisoned Glen, and Horn Head. In September they ferried their car to Scotland, where they again drove north and fulfilled one of

12   Una Jeffers, ca. 1936

Una's dreams—a tour of the Hebrides, Orkney, and Shetland Islands. From Cape Wrath they drove down through Scotland and England to London, where they stayed for two weeks. Excursions to places in central and southern England—such as Lord Byron's ancestral home, the grave of T. E. Lawrence, the grave of Mary Shelley, and the church where Thomas Hardy's heart is buried—completed their journey. They sailed for home October 30.

After landing in New York, they called on Edgar Lee Masters at his hotel, visited Bennett Cerf in his Random House office, spent a day with Edna St. Vincent Millay and her husband in their upstate country home, dined nearby with friends, and then drove on to Michigan to see Una's family. In late November they made their way to Taos for a two-week stay with Mabel and Tony Luhan. Then they drove to Palm Springs where they were guests at a ranch for two days. Finally, in mid-December, they returned to Carmel. "We arrived home in a wild storm," Una writes in a letter to Melba Bennett,

& oh how beautiful it was here.—We came into this dark house & began to sort ourselves out & unpack enough to go to bed with & to cook our supper & build fires—it was as if we had been gone ten minutes! How a house takes possession of one—one stretches out a hand in the dark—there exactly are the matches, a quarter turn—the stove & one doesn't even need a candle!

Una enjoyed herself throughout the journey, as did Garth and Donnan, but Robinson's experience, judging from comments made along the way, was not entirely positive. Writing Bennett Cerf from London early in October, Una says "Hard to tell how much or little R. J. has gotten out of our trip he is a miserable traveller." In a letter to Melba Bennett a few weeks later, she hints at continued difficulty: "Although he is certainly the world's worst traveller, Robin has survived to this point & I hope to get him home intact." Upon their return to Tor House in December, her report to Lawrence Clark Powell remains guarded: "Robin wrote only a few lines over in the British Isles but I think is much refreshed by his travels. I hope he will proceed on his way now."

Jeffers himself was more candid. In a letter to William van Wyck dated January 3, 1938, he says of his writing, "My own

13 West end of living room, Tor House, 1938

14 Una's alcove, east end of living room, Tor House, 1938

attempts don't amount to much at present—trifling things, and unlucky beginnings." The half-year away from home had not rejuvenated him. As he confides to van Wyck, expressing a need for complete oblivion, "I'd like to be buried for six years under deep forest by a waterside, not think, not remember, know nothing, see nothing but darkness, hear nothing but the river running for six years and the long roots growing, and then be resurrected. How fresh things would look."

Time and circumstance brought Jeffers back to where he was twenty years before, when, in the midst of the Great War, he struggled to find his way as an artist. His sons were two years old at that key moment in his life. He and Una were comfortably ensconced in a cabin by the sea. A dark cloud covered Jeffers, however, and he wrestled with thoughts of suicide. Now his sons were twenty-one, just the right age for uniform, and the world, Jeffers knew, was about to explode.

Despite Roosevelt's best efforts, the Depression returned in 1937. By 1938, with banks failing again, stocks lost 50 percent of their value, and 20 percent of the workforce was unemployed. The Spanish Civil War was raging. Japanese soldiers, having invaded China in July 1937, attacked Nanjing in December and, after capturing the city, unleashed a massacre that lasted through February 1938. In the middle of March, German troops entered Austria, and Hitler—in an act that shattered the Versailles Treaty—took possession of the country by annexation. In "Contemplation of the Sword," written in April 1938, Jeffers declares with certainty that "storms and counter-storms of general destruction" are on the world's horizon—"Reason will not decide at last:

the sword will decide." The thought of Garth and Donnan thrown into battle, along with all the other youths their age, filled him with dread—for the sword means horror: "loathsome disfigurements, blindness, mutilation, locked lips of boys / Too proud to scream."

Fear for the safety of his sons was compounded by a belief that he himself was about to die. Just before an Easter trip to Death Valley in April 1938, a trip that involved a flight in his brother's small airplane, Jeffers wrote a note to Una in which he shares a premonition borne in mind for several months. "On account of a dream I had in London," he says, "and a 'hunch' I have here, it seems to me possible that we may crash on the way to Death Valley, in spite of Hamilton's flying experience. Therefore this note, and the enclosed holograph last will and testament." The note includes instructions for the disposal of his body, along with related issues. "I have no prejudice against dying at any time—no desire to, but also no shrinking from it," he tells Una. "So you are not to mourn me if it should happen, but remember that I loved you dearly and wanted you and the boys to be happy, not sorrowful." Though the trip proceeded without incident, Jeffers' anxiety remained.

Jeffers was working on two memory-laden projects at this time. The first was a book of photographs of the Big Sur coast by Horace Lyon that, as conceived, would also feature excerpts from Jeffers' poems. As he studied the photographs for the proposed book, Jeffers saw the "seed-plots" for many of his narratives and recalled his first visit to the area—when, in December 1914, he, Una, and their dog Billie rode the mail stage 40 miles down the coast. His entire life as an artist was shaped by that experience. The second project was more substantial in size. Having decided it was time to publish a retrospective collection of Jeffers' verse, Bennett Cerf asked Jeffers to prepare *The Selected Poetry of Robinson Jeffers* (1938). In choosing poems for this book, Jeffers was forced to reevaluate everything he had ever written.

Both projects required forewords, and, in writing them, Jeffers took the opportunity to explain some of his goals as a poet, goals that differentiated him from other artists of his time. In the foreword to the book of photographs, for instance, he mentions "the cant we have heard about art," the cant that says "art must not be representational; it should not, if that were possible, even suggest nature; it should reject nature and produce its own forms, follow its own laws." This bias, of course, ran exactly counter to Jeffers' own convictions, which he affirms with reference to Lyon's realistic photographs of the Big Sur and his own narrative poetry. As he says of the latter, "each of my too many stories has grown up like a plant from some particular canyon or promontory, some particular relationship of rock and water, wood, grass and mountain."

In the foreword to *Selected Poetry* (which Jeffers completed in June 1938 and mailed to Random House from Taos), he makes a similar point. Returning, without mentioning it, to the period around December 1914 when mature ideas about poetry were forming in his mind, he says "it became evident to me that poetry—if it was to survive at all—must reclaim some of the power and reality it was so hastily surrendering to prose." Poetry written in French and English at that time "was becoming slight and fantastic, abstract, unreal, eccentric." To counter this tendency, Jeffers believed, poetry must "reclaim substance and sense, and physical and psychological reality"; it must "concern itself with (relatively) permanent things"; it must "deal with things that a reader two thousand years away could understand and be moved by." This conviction became the foundation for his own work. "It led me to write narrative poetry," he states, "and to draw subjects from contemporary life; to present aspects of life that modern poetry had generally avoided; and to attempt the expression of philosophic and scientific ideas in verse." It also compelled him to stand on his own, as Descartes did when he declared his commitment to skepticism. "I decided not to tell lies in verse," Jeffers says, "not to feign any emotion that I did not feel; not to pretend to believe in optimism or pessimism, or unreversible progress; not to say anything because it was popular, or generally accepted, or fashionable in intellectual circles, unless I myself believed it, and not to believe easily."

Two accidents, Jeffers adds, determined his destiny as an artist: meeting Una and moving to the Carmel coast, where life was primal. Una's influence, Jeffers declares, was crucial: "My nature is cold and undiscriminating; she excited and focused it, gave it eyes and nerves and sympathies. She never saw any of my poems until they were finished and typed, yet by her presence and conversation she has co-authored every one of them." He then offers a brief description: "She is more like a woman in a Scotch ballad, passionate, untamed and rather heroic—or like a falcon—than like any ordinary person."

Apparently, if Mabel Luhan is to be believed, Jeffers had the scars to prove it. In an unpublished memoir (mentioned in a January 2, 1938 letter from Una to Maud and Timmie Clapp), Mabel recounts a story Una told her in June 1938, soon after the Jeffers family arrived in Taos for their summer visit. Upon their return from the British Isles a few months before, Una confided, she and Robinson attended a Christmas party in the Carmel Highlands. On the way home, smoldering antagonisms burst into flame. When Jeffers stopped the car in a remote area, got out, and said "Let's end this *now*," Una thought he planned to kill her. With no defensive weapon at hand, she leaped forward and bit him on the neck, hoping to sever his jugular vein. With blood pouring from the wound, he grabbed her by the hair and tried to pull her away, but she held on, biting and scratching. "I suppose he could have knocked me out but he didn't," Una told Mabel,

I don't know why. I couldn't stop once I'd got started and we went on like that for two hours, at least until I was worn out. Then he said, you know, in that gentle way of his, "Shall we go home now, darling?" I looked at him then and you never *saw* such a wreck of a man. He was a *ruin*! He was bleeding all over—and his remaining clothes were covered with blood—wounds *everywhere*—gashes, streaks, bites! We drove home in complete silence. When we got to the house I washed him up as best I could but of course his evening clothes were ruined!

Though it is impossible to say if these events, as Mabel reports them, actually occurred, it *is* true that Robinson and Una were unstable when they arrived in Taos in the summer of 1938. Jeffers, having been restive for months, did not want to make the trip, but Mabel insisted, Una was so inclined, and Garth and Donnan always enjoyed New Mexico. The Jefferses arrived June 13, to be present at a trial in which Mabel was being sued for slander by a local doctor.

Soon after they settled in, two other guests joined the household—Dr. A. A. Brill and his wife Rose. In addition to being Mabel's psychiatrist, Dr. Brill was Sigmund Freud's translator and chief apologist in America. Random House had just published his Modern Library edition of *The Basic Writings of Sigmund Freud*. During meals and other times when they were all together, Brill drew everyone into an ongoing discussion of psychoanalysis. As might be expected, he focused attention on repression, wish fulfillment, and human sexuality, illustrating his insights with fascinating case histories.

After Brill and his wife departed, there was a letdown. This was lifted by the arrival, alone, of Hildegarde Donaldson, the unhappy wife of Norman Donaldson, director of Yale University Press. Hildegarde, a professional violinist in her early forties, was depressed because a long affair with a younger man had just ended. Robinson was immediately drawn to her, says Mabel, and Una instantly repelled. At sunrise one morning, when both were out walking because they could not sleep, Robinson and Hildegarde accidently met. As they awaited dawn together, Robinson confided his unhappiness, and a sympathetic bond was formed. A few nights later, Una accompanied Mabel on an errand, leaving Hildegarde, Robinson, and another guest talking by the fire. Hildegarde rose and left the room by one door; Robinson waited for a few minutes and left by another. He then made his way to her bedroom, where, without a word—according to Mabel—the two made love. When Una returned, Robinson was back in the living room, reading quietly.

Tension increased in the following days, with Robinson and Hildegarde seeking ways to spend time alone together and Una watching their every move. At one point, Una threatened violence if Hildegarde ever went after her husband. Another time, unable to control her suspicious rage, she twisted and scratched Hildegarde's arm. Unfriendly words exchanged between the two women included Hildegarde's charge that Una had broken Robinson with her jealousy and manic need for control.

On the evening of July 9, the night before Hildegarde was scheduled to leave, and after everyone had retired to their separate rooms, Mabel heard Jeffers' frantic voice: "Mabel! Mabel! Una's shot herself . . . come . . . come." After a long and bitter fight, Mabel later learned, Una had gone into the bathroom, swallowed a bottle of sleeping pills, got into the bathtub, pointed a revolver at her heart, and fired. When the doctor arrived, he found Hildegarde unconscious at the foot of a narrow flight of stairs. Having heard a call for help, she had rushed to Robinson's and Una's room and hit her head on a low beam. The doctor checked her quickly and then hurried up the stairs to Una; he found her in the tub, incoherent, blood pouring from her wound.

Una's stomach was pumped at the hospital, and she was operated on. The bullet had glanced off a rib, breaking it, and traveled beneath her skin around the ribcage, exiting from her back. They opened her side, cleaned the wound all along the bullet's path, and sewed her up again. After a few days, she was sent back to Mabel's, where she convalesced for two weeks before returning home. Jeffers wrote a few letters to Hildegarde, but the affair—or whatever it was—was over; he never saw her again.

At Tor House, Robinson and Una struggled to recover their equilibrium. Writing to Timmie and Maud Clapp August 7, 1938, just a few days after their twenty-fifth anniversary, Una reports on their progress. Robinson, she says,

has not been drinking any more but has been an angel of patience and needed to be! I've been very difficult. I have had days of dark melancholy, for my nerves are still a bit unstable: other days we have talked very quietly & sensibly about his difficulty writing and I think we have hit upon a few plans to ease that up. There have been days when I was such a whirlwind of anger & resentment that I have almost blown the roof off & us through it! And other times of such tempestuous love-making—as if this menace to our life together forced us to express to its extreme bounds the passion which we have always felt for each other. Not a very restful period.

Writing to the Clapps again a month later, Una describes the situation somewhat differently, this time with Robinson as the focus of concern. "What of our household," she says, as if responding to a question,

—halcyon days of happiness & calm, sometimes ten days at a time, even two weeks. Then a twenty four hours of *incredible* horror. At last just now after one of these spells, certain developments—& understandings seem to point to peace & renewals. It is hard for me to keep on being bored & angry—I think I shall soon be as gay as a lark if calm reigns.

"I wish he were as resilient," she adds. "At least I feel now the intensity of his love as well as the extent [of] his brutality. He has seemed like Heathcliffe in *Wuthering Heights*—remember? Savage." As the months passed, physical and emotional wounds began to heal, but both Robinson and Una remained unsteady.

—Unsteady as the world. In "Nerves," a poem written in February 1939, Jeffers speaks of heightened tension everywhere. "Few minds now are quite sane," he observes; "nearly every person / Seems to be listening for a crash, listening . . . / And *wishing* for it, with a kind of enraged / Sensibility." In "The Soul's Desert," dated August 30, 1939, two days before Germany invaded Poland and four days before Britain and France declared war, Jeffers refers to the empty but dangerous rhetoric of government leaders, heard many times before. "They are warming up the old horrors," he declares, "and all that they say is echoes of echoes." Three weeks later, with the occupation of Poland nearly complete, with tens of thousands of people dead or in captivity, and with the Soviet Union's collusion with Germany revealed, the long-expected crash had come. On September 19, 1939, Hitler gave a belligerent speech in Danzig, which Jeffers heard, as delivered, via radio.

In "The Day Is a Poem," written in response, Jeffers describes Hitler as "A man of genius: that is, of amazing /

15 Robinson Jeffers, 1940

Ability, courage, devotion, cored on a sick child's soul." In the fierce barking of the *Führer*—the "dog-wrath," as Jeffers calls it—one could hear, clearly, the voice of "a sick child / Wailing in Danzig; invoking destruction and wailing at it." Carmel that day was extremely hot. Around noon, Jeffers reports, a south wind brought light rain. Later, an earthquake shook Tor House. Later still, in the dark of night, a blood-red moon dropped slowly "Into black sea through bursts of dry lightning and distant thunder." Through it all, Jeffers listened and watched, concluding finally that the day was a poem, but too much like one of his own: "crusted with blood and barbaric omens, / Painful to excess, inhuman as a hawk's cry."

1940–1945

In February 1941, Jeffers embarked on a trip unlike any he had taken before. Deferring to Una's judgment in the matter, Jeffers accepted an invitation to participate in a program titled "The Poet in a Democracy" presented by the Library of Congress in Washington, D.C. The event, the first of its kind at the library, was arranged by Joseph Auslander under the direction of poet and librarian Archibald MacLeish. Jeffers was asked to be the inaugural speaker in the series of readings, with Robert Frost, Carl Sandburg, and Stephen Vincent Benét scheduled for later dates. Since he and Una planned to drive by automobile across the country, Jeffers also accepted invitations to speak at other places: the University of Pittsburgh on the way to Washington; Harvard, Princeton, Columbia, the State University of New York at Buffalo, Butler University, the University of Kansas City, and the University of Utah on the way home. For Jeffers, who had never spoken at length in public nor read his poetry aloud to a general audience, this was a major milestone.

Except for blizzards encountered along the way, one of which forced the cancellation of the reading at Princeton, the 8,000-mile journey was a success. In Washington, Robinson and Una were the guests of Eugene Meyer, owner of the *Washington Post*, and his wife Agnes. The audience at the Library of Congress—which included Supreme Court justices, cabinet officers, government workers, and readers of all ages—was so large that, after the auditorium filled, arrangements were made for people to hear Jeffers through loudspeakers in an adjoining room. When that room overflowed as well, more than 200 people were turned away.

Jeffers began his talk with a statement concerning democracy in America. "Our democracy has provided, and still provides," he said, "the greatest freedom for the greatest number of people. That is its special glory." He then discussed the difference between Athens and Sparta in ancient Greece, the crisis in modern Europe, and America's role as a guardian of Western values. After sharing his thoughts about the current war—which America had not yet officially entered—and illustrating them with relevant poems, Jeffers turned to other subjects: mythology, the Big Sur coast, Una, Ireland, and death. The last subject offered Jeffers an opportunity to address a misconception. "I have heard myself called a pessimist," he said, "and perhaps I have written some words of ill omen in my books of verses; and perhaps I have spoken to-night some words of ill omen:—but they are not words of despair." With reference to "Antrim," a poem about death and rebirth he had just read, Jeffers said "I think that when poetry dreams too much about death, there is always a resurrection being plotted." He then concluded his presentation with a sober but uplifting message:

If we conjecture the decline and fall of this civilization, it is because we hope for a better one. We are a tough race, we human beings; we have lived through an ice-age and many ages of barbarism; we can live through this age of civilization; and when at length it wears out and crumbles under us, we can "plot our agony of resurrection" and make a new age. Our business is, to live. To live *through* . . . anything. And to keep alive, through everything, our ideal values, of freedom and courage, and mercy and tolerance.

A reception at the Meyer home attended by Alice Roosevelt Longworth and other dignitaries followed the reading. The next day, a story published in the *Washington Post* bore an enthusiastic headline: "Poetry Series Well Begun, Library Officials Are Jubilant." In describing Jeffers, the author of the story refers to the "poet's shy, friendly smile," the music of his "slow rolling voice," and his "grave, kindly" manner. While Robinson and Una were in Washington, a variety of activities were planned for them, including trips to Mt. Vernon and Arlington, a private tour of the Supreme Court led by Harlan Stone, soon to be named chief justice, and, for

Jeffers alone, a formal dinner with such men as William S. Knudsen, who resigned his position as president of General Motors in order to direct Roosevelt's war production effort.

Robinson and Una were treated with equal courtesy in Cambridge, New York, Buffalo, and the other cities on their itinerary. In "Themes in My Poems," the presentation he prepared for university audiences, he used some of the material from his Washington speech, augmented with a discussion of major themes found in his poems—such as death, war, the rise and fall of civilizations, strain within the European–American worldview, human narcissism, the beauty of the universe, the self-inflicted suffering of God, the California coast, and the majesty of hawks. "Another theme that has much engaged my verses," Jeffers said at one point, providing a key to his work as a whole,

is the expression of a religious feeling, that perhaps must be called pantheism, though I hate to type it with a name. It is the feeling . . . I will say the certainty . . . that the universe is one being, a single organism, one great life that includes all life and all things; and is so beautiful that it must be loved and reverenced; and in moments of mystical vision we identify with it.

Upon their return home from this trip, Jeffers resumed work on his next book. Perhaps with Othello's confused explanation for his own murderous behavior in mind, Jeffers thought of calling it *The Cause.* He also considered *Give Nature Time*, *This Pallid Comet*, *The Bloody Sire*, *Never Weep*, and *The Stars Fly Over.* These titles were all rejected in favor of *Be*

Angry at the Sun. Jeffers sent the finished manuscript to Random House in May and corrected proofs in July.

Be Angry at the Sun and Other Poems was released in October 1941. In a prefatory note, Jeffers laments "the obsession with contemporary history" that pins many of the poems to the calendar. Along with "Contemplation of the Sword," "Nerves," "The Soul's Desert," and "The Day Is a Poem," mentioned previously, the book contains other poems that refer to specific days or events, such as "Moon and Five Planets," a poem about the Winter War in Finland written March 10, 1940, and "Battle," a poem about conditions of life in wartime dated May 28, 1940, the day Belgium surrendered to Germany. "Poetry is not private monologue," Jeffers asserts in his note, but "it is not public speech either; and in general it is the worse for being timely." Nevertheless, he adds,

it is right that a man's views be expressed, though the poetry suffer for it. Poetry should represent the whole mind; if part of the mind is occupied unhappily, so much the worse. And no use postponing the poetry to a time when these storms may have passed, for I think we have but seen a beginning of them; the calm to look for is the calm at the whirlwind's heart.

The first poem in the book, *Mara*, is set in the Big Sur and tells a familiar story. Bruce and Allen Ferguson, brothers and ranchers, live in the Ferguson family home with their parents—a dying father and an old, bitter mother—and Bruce's wife Fawn and daughter. Bruce, a casually unfaithful husband, suspects that his wife and brother are having an affair.

He is right about this, but he suffers a mental breakdown before obtaining certain proof and hangs himself. Meanwhile, old Mrs. Ferguson, filled with a lifetime of anger, kills her husband with an overdose of morphine. Throughout the story, events in Europe provide background and counterpoint. In one instance, as midnight comes to the Big Sur and dawn arrives in Europe, Bruce, in a jealous, drunken rage, attacks a man at a country dance; at the same moment, on the other side of the world, Hitler invades Poland. "The cause is far beyond good and evil," Jeffers says of these and similar events; "Men fight and their cause is not the cause." In the aftermath, with the mother's crime concealed, Bruce dead, and Europe flaming, Allen and Fawn begin their life together, certain of their right to happiness.

The second work in *Be Angry at the Sun* is a one-act verse drama, a masque titled *The Bowl of Blood*. The setting is a fisherman's cabin in northern Germany occupied by a simple woman known for her skills as a spiritual medium. Three disembodied beings, called Maskers, are present at the cabin when Hitler, hoping to learn his future, and two attendants arrive for a séance. After breathing vapors from a bowl of blood placed on a stool before her, the woman enters a trance, at which time the Maskers appear and speak—one as Frederick the Great, another as Napoleon. Both of these leaders prove unnerving to Hitler, Napoleon especially. The third Masker then enters the room as Ernst Friedenau, a friend of Hitler who died during World War I. Friedenau forecasts victory for Hitler; in due time, he prophesies, Holland, Flanders, France, and England, like Poland and

Czechoslovakia, will fall. "I see your war-engines / Rip the enemy front to ribbons, like screaming flesh under a meat-mincer," he says; "I see the poplar-lined roads / Packed with fugitives, your planes rake them from the air, your heartless machines crush them in ditches." These words excite Hitler but also fill him with dread. "*I did not want this war*," he utters, wringing his hands like Pilate. One of the Maskers agrees, saying in a voice the humans cannot hear and moving in a shape they cannot see (a skeleton performing a *Totentanz*), "Oh, yes, they all share the guilt / All the governments, all the great nations stand / With blood on their hands"—including America.

As the séance draws to a close, the Masker who speaks as Friedenau urges Hitler on, claiming he will soon be as famous as Caesar or Charlemagne. "I believe. I believe. I *will* believe," says Hitler, despite forebodings of utter destruction. At this point, the medium returns to normal consciousness, knocking the bowl to the floor as she does so. Hitler recoils from the pool of blood that gathers at his feet, but then regains composure. He leaves the cabin like a sleepwalker, "half conscious of the future," ready to play his role in the tragic drama unfolding about him.

Other poems in *Be Angry at the Sun*, like the doom-laden lyrics already mentioned, speak of current events with stoic resignation. "Violence has been the sire of all the world's values," Jeffers ruefully observes in one poem, and "All will be worse confounded soon," he proclaims in another.

On December 7, 1941, just a few weeks after *Be Angry at the Sun* was published, Japan attacked Pearl Harbor. This, for

America, marked the official beginning of World War II. Joining Britain, France, the Soviet Union, and more than a dozen other countries in a confederation called the Allies, the United States faced an Axis coalition composed of Germany, Italy, Japan, and their supporters. At just that moment in history when science and technology reached an entirely new peak, giving humans unprecedented control over natural forces, all efforts in the Machine Age seemed to turn toward death. On air and land and sea, fighter planes and bombers, armored cars and tanks, submarines and battleships—all newly designed and mass-produced—carried their cargoes of men and mechanized weapons around the world. By the time the war was over in August 1945, whole countries were in ruin, and over 50,000,000 soldiers and civilians were dead. Tens of millions more were wounded.

Carmel was closer to the war than most places in America. After the attack on Pearl Harbor, there were widespread worries about an invasion along the California coast. Military units were deployed to guard the area, and civilians were asked to watch the sea and sky. Moreover, Fort Ord, one of America's most important military facilities, was located on the dunes north of Monterey. At its peak, 50,000 soldiers at a time were placed in infantry, field artillery, engineering, and medical units there, as they learned everything from hand-to-hand combat to amphibious assault. The base also housed a large hospital for wounded veterans and a prison for enemy combatants. Men and women in uniform filled the streets of every community nearby.

Jeffers deplored war in principle, particularly those fought in his lifetime, but he understood war's place in human existence and accepted the necessity of defensive combat. Una was more martial. As America mobilized after Pearl Harbor, her New Year's toast for 1942 was "May we be staunch and resourceful this year, and *as Ruthless as Necessary!*" For his part, Jeffers studied airplane identification and manned a lookout post in the Carmel Highlands, sometimes from midnight to dawn. Una worked tirelessly at Fort Ord as a Red Cross volunteer, eventually chairing the hospital Staff Assistance Corps.

After their marital problems in 1938, the two faced discord for a time. Their emotions were again strained in late 1941, just before *Be Angry at the Sun* was published, when Una was diagnosed with cancer and underwent a mastectomy. For a brief moment in the following year, Jeffers turned to another woman—Connie Flavin, an actress and family friend who lived nearby. In time, however, he and Una found their way back to each other and, as the war progressed, reaffirmed their love. Their two sons, now grown, began their own lives away from home. Garth, after completing his university education, worked for more than a year as a cowhand on a large ranch in New Mexico. Donnan, who did not finish his degree, married and moved to Ohio. A slight heart murmur was discovered during Donnan's draft physical, so he was never called for duty. Garth was judged physically fit and was inducted in April 1942. Assigned to a Military Police combat battalion, he entered advanced commando training and served in the Pacific and Europe, eventually earning battle stars with General Patton's Third Army in Germany.

Jeffers was one of the few American poets of his generation who had a son in harm's way for the duration of the war—which might explain why he held his breath and published only one book. Jeffers continued to write, however, and contributed poems to anthologies edited between 1940 and 1945 by Oscar Williams. Despite the call from poets like Archibald MacLeish for American writers to get behind the war effort, Jeffers, true to his convictions, determinedly opposed it. From his perspective, Americans were drawn into war by dishonest leaders. As Jeffers observes in "Pearl Harbor," one of the poems published in Williams' *New Poems: 1944*, "Here are the fireworks. The men who conspired and labored / To embroil this republic in the wreck of Europe have got their bargain— / And a bushel more." Addressing his own Hawk Tower, built at the end of World War I, he takes stock of the destruction in both general and particular terms. "Look," he says with pity and sarcasm, "This dust blowing is only the British Empire; these torn leaves flying / Are only Europe; the wind is the plane-propellers; the smoke is Tokyo. The child with the butchered throat / Was too young to be named." No matter how noble the cause (or how noble war is made out to be by those who want it), war of the sort then being waged was an abomination—as Jeffers argues in "Calm and Full the Ocean," also published in Williams' 1944 anthology.

Calm and full the ocean under the cool dark sky; quiet rocks and the
    birds fishing; the night-herons
Have flown home to their wood . . . while east and west in Europe and
    Asia and the islands unimaginable agonies

Consume mankind. Not a few thousand but uncounted millions, not a
day but years, pain, horror, sick hatred;
Famine that dries the children to little bones and huge eyes; high
explosive that fountains dirt, flesh and bone-splinters.

Sane and intact the seasons pursue their course, autumn slopes to
December, the rains will fall
And the grass flourish, with flowers in it: as if man's world were
perfectly separate from nature's, private and mad.

In "Eagle Valor, Chicken Mind," a poem built on an image
that almost seems humorous, Jeffers praises the American
people for their strength, their "eagle wings and beak." In
his estimation, however, the nation was governed by people
with "chicken brains"—small and even cowardly. "Weep (it
is frequent in human affairs)," he says, "weep for the terrible
magnificence of the means, / The ridiculous incompetence
of the reasons, the bloody and shabby / Pathos of the result."

Jeffers was the only major American poet of his generation
writing verse like this at the time. T. S. Eliot's *Four Quartets*, one
of the greatest works of the 1940s, refers obliquely to the war,
but the suite as a whole is primarily concerned with self-inte-
gration and Christian redemption. H. D., while more directly
concerned with the war itself in *Trilogy*, also sets the search
for understanding within a biblical frame, as does Marianne
Moore in "'Keeping Their World Large'" and "In Distrust
of Merits." Wallace Stevens addresses wartime conditions in
"Dry Loaf," "Martial Cadenza," "Esthétique du Mal," and
other poems, but given his preference for abstraction and his

belief that poets should "resist or evade" the pressure of reality, his observations are inspired by, but disengaged from, immediate conditions. Despite William Carlos Williams' claim in his introduction to *The Wedge* (1944) that "war is the first and only thing in the world today" and that his book does not turn away ("It *is* the war or part of it, merely a different sector of the field"), poems in *The Wedge* have little to do with the war itself. Most are informed by the sentiment found in "War, the Destroyer!" written for Martha Graham and published in 1942: "What is war, / the destroyer / but an appurtenance / to the dance? / The deadly serious / who would have us suppress / all exuberance / because of it / are mad. When terror blooms— / leap and twist / whirl and prance— / that's the show / of this the circumstance."

Like Williams, E. E. Cummings also chose to work in a different sector of the field. Most of the poems in *1 × 1* (1944) are concerned with "what over and which under / burst lurch things phantom curl" and other matters. Robert Frost responded to current events in a similar fashion. The book he published during wartime, *A Witness Tree* (1942), contains one direct reference to the war—in "November" Frost refers to "The waste of nations warring"—but the book as a whole deals with homelier subjects. Edna St. Vincent Millay and Carl Sandburg were openly partisan and propagandistic in *The Murder of Lidice* and "The Man with the Broken Fingers," both of which provide vivid descriptions of German cruelty. In a similar vein, Archibald MacLeish wrote essays and delivered speeches in support of the Allied cause—such as "The Irresponsibles" and "The Country of the Mind

Must Also Attack," published in *A Time to Speak* (1940) and *A Time to Act* (1943). Propaganda for the Axis effort was provided by Ezra Pound in radio broadcasts from Rome. From 1941 to 1943, prior to his arrest for treason, he repeatedly praised Hitler and Mussolini, denounced Roosevelt and Churchill, and excoriated Jews.

There was, of course, no "right" way to respond to the destruction as it unfolded, and for the most part, despite broad differences of opinion, modern poets honored the autonomy and integrity of artistic vision. Though some critics denounced Jeffers for his political convictions, he was still held in high esteem. As a member since 1937 of the National Institute of Arts and Letters, an honorary association incorporated by an act of Congress and limited to 250 distinguished American artists, musicians, and writers, Jeffers was eligible for membership in the even more exclusive American Academy of Arts and Letters. The academy, established within the institute in 1904, was composed of just fifty luminaries, each preeminent in his or her field. Early members of the academy included Henry Adams, William Merritt Chase, Joel Chandler Harris, Winslow Homer, Julia Ward Howe, Henry James, Edward MacDowell, John Muir, Theodore Roosevelt, John Singer Sargent, Mark Twain, and Woodrow Wilson. When chairs became vacant in the academy, members selected new honorees from the institute's rolls. Jeffers was chosen in November 1945. In the following month, the Academy of American Poets honored Jeffers with an invitation to serve on its first Board of Chancellors.

These honors were bestowed in the months following V-E (Victory in Europe) and V-J (Victory over Japan) Days, May 8 and August 15, 1945. The United States was rapidly demobilizing at this time, with millions of soldiers returning home to begin new lives in a changed America: an America with no unemployment, higher wages than before the war, a better standard of living for virtually everyone, ongoing urban and industrial development, towering stature in the world community of nations, and shared pride in a job well done. For the "good life" and "a better world"—with Big Band music swinging on the radio and filling the USO canteens, with buxom pin-ups painted on the noses of the bombers, and with confidence in the holiness of the task—Americans faced their enemies and won.

They did so with sheer brute force. The depth of American fury was revealed in a Gallup poll administered in November 1944. Thirteen percent of respondents—when asked "What do you think we should do with Japan, as a country, after the war?"—recommended genocide: "Kill all Japanese people," they said. Another 33 percent answered "Destroy as a political entity." Most likely, if the same question had been asked of the military, the percentages would have been greater. Indeed, at about the same time as the poll was taken, high-altitude bombing of Japan began. At first, aircraft manufacturing plants were the primary targets. By March 1945, as a result of successes throughout the Pacific theater, the skies were safe enough for low-altitude missions. For ten days in the middle of the month, according to a United States government summary report, Americans flew

1,600 sorties and dropped nearly 19,000,000 pounds of explosives on Tokyo, Nagoya, Osaka, and Kobe, setting each city aflame. In the attack on Tokyo alone, 15 square miles of the city were destroyed and 185,000 men, women, and children either burned to death or suffered serious wounds. At the end of March, Operation Starvation began. As inland waterways and harbors were sown with mines and 670 ships were sunk, food supplies stopped moving and industrial production ceased.

With the islands of Japan now dead in the water, and with no significant defense, a more extensive bombing campaign was initiated. By July 1945, 208,000,000 pounds of explosives fell on 66 urban areas, burning factories, arsenals, oil refineries, airfields, and more than 2,500,000 family homes. On average, 40 percent of each city disappeared. In August, just three weeks after tests were completed in New Mexico, atomic bombs were dropped on Hiroshima and Nagasaki, to devastating consequence. A few days later, with conditional peace terms on the table, bombers carrying conventional weapons attacked Tokyo again. By the time the nine-month bombing campaign was over—and with it, the war as a whole—over 800,000 Japanese civilians were dead or wounded, and the country, from Kagoshima to Aomori, was burned to the ground. Just after the event, with accounts of the explosions filling newspapers across the land, Americans were asked if the use of atomic weapons on civilian targets was justified. Eighty-five percent said yes.

IV. EAGLE AND HAWK

Eagle and hawk with their great claws and hooked heads
Tear life to pieces; vulture and raven wait for death to soften it.
The poet cannot feed on this time of the world
Until he has torn it to pieces, and himself also.

Circa 1957—from an untitled poem fragment

1945–1950

When World War II officially ended, waves of euphoria swept the land. Jeffers did not celebrate. He was grateful his son Garth came through the war unharmed, but at deeper levels, where thoughts concerning America, Western Civilization, and human nature as a whole reside, he was appalled. His revulsion was like that of other artists in previous centuries faced with similar carnage. One thinks of Francisco de Goya, for example, who, in the Napoleonic Era, recorded his anguish in a series of etchings titled *Disasters of War* and in such paintings as *Saturn Devouring One of His Children, Duel with Cudgels*, and *The Third of May, 1808*.

Perhaps, if one brings the *Saturn* painting to mind, it is understandable why Jeffers turned so readily to a project brought to him by a drama producer. In February 1945, Jed Harris contacted Jeffers with a request for a new translation of *Medea*, with Judith Anderson already selected for the title role. The play, like Goya's painting of Saturn, depicts a horrific instance of infanticide—a fitting symbol for the destructiveness of war.

Jeffers may have been attracted to the project for several other reasons, including a feeling of kinship with Euripides, the last of the great Greek tragedians. Like Jeffers, Euripides matured as an artist during a time of war—the Peloponnesian War in his case. Known for his preference for solitude and for the psychological realism of his work, Euripides questioned the pieties of his time, denounced demagogues and dishonest politicians, and examined, without blinking, the fact of human cruelty and the mystery of suffering, especially in such searing anti-war plays as *Andromache*, *Hecuba*, and *The Trojan Women*. Jeffers may also have been drawn to the project because of Medea's similarity to many of his own female characters—women, such as Tamar, who live beyond the reach of civilized conventions and do whatever is necessary to get what they want. Another reason for Jeffers' interest may have involved Judith Anderson. Already famous for her portrayals of Lady Macbeth, Queen Gertrude, and other formidable women, Anderson was known to Jeffers from her performance of Clytemnestra in a 1941 Carmel production of *The Tower Beyond Tragedy*, Jeffers' adaptation of Aeschylus' *Oresteia* first published in *Roan Stallion, Tamar and Other Poems*. Having seen her on stage speaking words he had written, he knew what she could do with the part of Medea. In any case, the proposal gripped Jeffers; he set aside the narrative poem he was working on and turned immediately to Euripides' play.

The finished script, titled *Medea: Freely Adapted from the Medea of Euripides*, was published by Random House early in 1946. The publication of the book was supposed to coincide with the opening of the play, but Jed Harris withdrew and the production collapsed. Anderson kept the project alive, however, and, after a series of false starts, rehearsals for a Broadway production of *Medea* began.

Several other projects came to fruition at the same time. Early in October 1947, a production of *Dear Judas* opened on Broadway. This event was accompanied by an essay about the play written by Jeffers and published as "Preface to 'Judas'" in the *New York Times*. Later in October, *Medea* premiered. Three months after that, in January 1948, the *New York Times* published an essay by Jeffers titled "Poetry, Góngorism, and a Thousand Years." Then, in July 1948, soon after *Medea* ended its long run, one of Jeffers' most controversial books was released—*The Double Axe and Other Poems*. Two Broadway productions, two essays in a leading newspaper, and a major book, all appearing within a few months' time, delivered an unequivocal message: Americans looking for praise and reassurance after the Good War, as World War II came to be called, were not going to get it from Jeffers.

The production of *Dear Judas* was conceived by Michael Myerberg, owner of the Mansfield Theatre on Broadway. Jeffers himself was not involved in any way. Stiff resistance came as soon as Myerberg announced his intention to mount a trial run at the Ogunquit Playhouse in Maine. A local citizen asked the playhouse to reject the play, arguing that its content was "revolting to a Christian." The production, starring E. G. Marshall in the title role, proceeded on schedule, but the response was negative and clearly touched a nerve. "Those who suspected its religious propriety had their suspicions confirmed," said one reviewer, siding with detractors; the play "offered nothing to a world that needs more faith instead of less." Myerberg encountered more resistance when he tried to open the play in Boston. The mayor of the city, working in concert with Catholic churchmen, declared his intent to ban *Dear Judas*, arguing that showing the play would "violate the beliefs of many Bostonians in God, and might even create trouble by stirring up religious feeling."

The outcry against the play was rooted in what the public already knew about Jeffers' critical attitude toward Christ and Christianity. The play itself, available to readers for nearly twenty years, portrayed Mary and Jesus in all-too-human terms—as a mother and son unable to face the illegitimate birth that binds them. The lie they shared, that Jesus was a miracle-child fathered by God, became an obsession with Jesus and a matter of faith for his deluded followers. Jeffers makes the same point in other poems, as in "Theory of Truth" where he says that Jesus' "personal anguish and insane solution / Have stained an age; nearly two thousand years are one vast poem drunk with the wine of his blood." Indeed, Jeffers says in *Mara*, there are "no angels and no devils" behind the decline of civilization and the savagery of modern times, for "Christ unopposed would corrupt all."

During World War I, Jeffers wrote a poem titled "The Beginning of Decadence" in which he condemned "Churches that were selling God for silver and when a war began /

Blessed the bayonets and praised manslaughter in the name of the Son of Man." This sentiment, which stayed with Jeffers through the years, stood against and undercut the presumptions of one of the most popular songs of World War II—"Praise the Lord and Pass the Ammunition," a song about a navy chaplain who lays aside his Bible and starts firing a big gun. "Praise the Lord, we're on a mighty mission!" the chaplain shouts, "All aboard, we're not a-goin' fishin; / Praise the Lord and pass the ammunition and we'll all stay free!" Such a song, for Jeffers, was nothing more than a symptom of cultural decay. For this reason, as he looked to the far distant future and imagined a primitive world without civilization or the church, he could only hope for a poet who would warn people against witch doctors and urge them "if any man says / 'I am a priest,' to kill them with spears" ("Hellenistics").

No wonder devout believers, especially clergymen, were incensed. By the time *Dear Judas* was ready to open in New York, Myerberg knew for certain the play was in trouble. In a last-ditch effort to save the production, he asked Jeffers to explain his original intentions. Jeffers complied, and an essay titled "Preface to 'Judas'" was printed in the *New York Times* on opening night, October 5, 1947.

Jeffers begins the essay by saying he never imagined *Dear Judas* staged and that he was surprised by the opposition to its production in Maine and Boston. The verse drama was written, he explains, "like other poems of mine, because the great passions that produced some significant event came visibly into my mind and sought expression." In this case, the passions were those of Mary, Jesus, and Judas, and the significant event was the birth of Christianity. To understand both, Jeffers asserts, it is important to put aside sentimentalism when reading the gospels and to look directly at the tormented human beings involved. Jesus, for instance, is more than the "mere incarnation of love" that many people see. A close reading of the objective narrative reveals a mind that is "deep, powerful and beautiful; and strangely complex, not wholly integrated. He is the Prince of Peace, and yet He came 'not to bring peace but a sword.' He is gentle and loving, yet He drives men with whips from the temple, He calls down destruction on Jerusalem, His curse kills a fig tree." In the same way, Judas is more than he seems. While the narrative tradition reduces him to a stock figure, a traitor driven by lust for money, it also reveals that "he had been accepted among Christ's disciples; his despair at the end was so deep that he threw back the silver . . . and went and hanged himself." Given the scant but suggestive information provided in the gospels, one is left free, Jeffers argues, to imagine Judas' mind, "provided only that it tallies with his acts; and I have imagined it as skeptical, humanitarian, pessimistic and sick with pity."

Seen from this perspective, Judas' betrayal of Jesus, who appeared to his friend to be drifting toward madness, was really an act of love, and Jesus' love, rooted in a desire to possess his followers, was, in truth, an act of betrayal. Jesus "deliberately sought crucifixion because He understood that only a fierce and dreadful symbol could capture the minds of a fierce people. Only the cross, and death by torture, could 'fill the wolf bowels of Rome'; and conquer the blond savages from the North, who were about to take over Rome's power and primacy." "No man shall live," Jesus says in the play, "as if *I* had not lived."

In crafting the drama, Jeffers sought simplicity, choosing "the method of the Japanese Noh plays, which present a haunted place and passion's afterglow, two or three ghosts or echoes of life, re-enacting in a dream their ancient deeds and sorrows." Myerberg pushed the material further, adding pageantry, puppetry, dance, and music, with Bach chorales sung throughout. "'Dear Judas' is iconoclastic and anti-scriptural and it is also very tedious and undramatic," said one reviewer; it is "the profane translation of a sacred story, arty, pretentious and uncalled for," said another. The production fell flat and closed October 18, 1947 after sixteen performances.

Medea, directed by John Gielgud (who also played Jason) and starring Judith Anderson, opened on Broadway two nights later, October 20, 1947. Robinson and Una flew to New York for the premiere. Like everyone else in the audience, they were overwhelmed by Anderson's performance. Thunderous applause required thirteen curtain calls. At one point, Jeffers also took a bow.

In reviews published the following day, both poet and actress were praised. "Using a new text by Robinson Jeffers," said one reviewer, Judith Anderson "set a landmark in the theatre at the National last evening, where she gave a burning performance in a savage part." Jeffers' adaptation, the reviewer adds, "spares the supernatural bogeymen of the classical Greek drama and gets on briskly with the terrifying story of a woman obsessed with revenge. His verse is modern; his words are sharp and vivid, and his text does not worship gods that are dead."

Other reviews contain similar observations: "The simple, direct, striking and eloquent verse" of Jeffers' *Medea* "is both dramatically and poetically satisfying"; "*Medea* provides an evening of sustained horror . . . but it also has dignity and eloquence. There is a beauty of language in the Robinson Jeffers adaptation, and Miss Anderson is always there to keep the excitement at a high pitch"; Anderson's "Medea is overwhelming; it knocks you down"; "This role begins on a pitch of great emotional intensity. It rises to heights that surpass endurance"; "It does what only the stage—and only the stage when involved with high drama—can do to assault and inflame and exhaust the emotions"; "unfaltering magnificence"; "an onlooker is left stunned and numb"; "Here is a performance of such scope and forcefulness, of such boldness of imagination, that it is not likely to be forgotten by anyone who witnesses it."

When *Medea* was first staged in 431 BCE, Athenians must have shifted uneasily in their seats, not just because of the violence depicted on stage but because of the way some aspects of Medea's story illuminated current events. One of the precipitating causes of the Peloponnesian War (which began in 431 BCE), as Thucydides notes, was conflict between Corinth and Athens over the island of Corcyra (Corfu). Corinth, an ally of Sparta, had a long history of hating Athens—a history rooted in myth, as Euripides reminds his audience in his play. The story of *Medea* takes place in Corinth, where the sorceress and her husband settled after completing their adventures with the Golden Fleece. When Jason decides he no longer needs Medea, he arranges to marry Creüsa, King Creon's daughter. In response, Medea plots revenge. After extracting a blind promise of safe haven from Aegeus, the king of Athens, in exchange for a cure for his sterility, Medea burns Creüsa alive in a golden cloak, murders Creon, who is caught up in his daughter's flames, and slits her two sons' throats. She then mounts a chariot and speeds to Athens, with the wounded rage of Corinth at her back. For the Athenians who first saw the play, the distinction between mythic and actual time would have been suspended. Because of Aegeus' promise and despite Corinth's anger (against which Athenians had to stiffen), Medea was theirs to protect; at that moment, she was on her way to their town.

In 1947, nearly two-and-a-half millennia later, Jeffers told his audience, in effect, that once Medea reached Athens—a fountainhead of Western glory and a source of America's greatness—she never left. Along with democracy, the Parthenon, Plato, Aristotle, and all the rest, the Dark Mother was part of civilization, as, through the centuries, evidence of her cold-blooded fury attests. Furthermore, though Jeffers never makes a direct connection between Aegeus and Roosevelt, he no doubt saw a similarity. As emasculated rulers, one afflicted with sterility (some say impotence) and the other a "cripple's-power-need," they both gave Medea free rein.

Audiences may not have fully understood the original cultural context for *Medea* or grasped all of Jeffers' intentions, but they felt the play's power. One New York reviewer, writing for the *Los Angeles Times*, praised Anderson—and, behind her, Jeffers—for "crowding into two hours the accumulated bitterness, savagery and ferocity of the world." For post-war theatergoers still striving to assimilate recent events, the play proved cathartic. Seats filled night after night, and *Medea* was a major hit. After more than 200 performances on Broadway, for which Anderson won a Tony Award, she assembled a touring company and performed the role over 300 more times in cities across the country. She finished the tour with a return to Broadway in May 1949, still to great acclaim.

Two months into the run, Jeffers was invited by editors of the *New York Times* to contribute an essay on poetry to their Sunday magazine. The result, titled "Poetry, Góngorism, and a Thousand Years," appeared January 18, 1948. "The present is a time of high civilization rapidly declining," Jeffers says near the outset; "it is not a propitious period for any of the arts." Nevertheless, he argues, great poetry is still possible if a poet avoids the paths laid out by Rimbaud and Hopkins, realizes that Eliot's *Waste Land*, as impressive as it is, "marks the close of a literary dynasty, not the beginning," and turns away from "the self-consciousness and naive learnedness, the undergraduate irony, unnatural metaphors, hiatuses and labored obscurity that are too prevalent in contemporary verse."

In previous centuries and other cultures, Jeffers observes, poets like Luis de Góngora y Argote (1561–1627) composed poetry intended for an intellectual elite. In his case, that meant "a jargon of dislocated constructions and far-fetched metaphors, self-conscious singularity, studious obscurity." Góngora was popular for a time, but his work soon fell out of favor. "Euphuism in England"—the ornate and artificial style of John Lyly (1554?–1606) and his imitators—"had a similar vogue and a similar catastrophe." The "more extreme tendencies of modernist verse," Jeffers adds, "are diseases of like nature, later forms of Góngorism; doctrinaire corruptions of instinct."

The collapse of taste observed in modern art generally, where "sculpture (for instance) may sink to fiddling with bits of wire and tin trinkets," creates time-bound work with limited appeal. A great poet of the modern era, on the other hand, would be "natural and direct"; he (or she) would ignore "the neon lights and toothpaste advertising of this urban civilization, and the momentary popular imbecilities"; he would "distrust the fashionable poetic dialect" of the era and avoid the "studiously quaint and difficult." A great poet, in short, would not write like the major modernists or their younger acolytes. He would write like Euripides, Yeats, or any other poet who speaks for his own time and all time. "Great poetry is pointed at the future. Its author, whether consciously or not, intends to be understood a thousand years from now; therefore he chooses the more permanent aspects of things, and subjects that will remain valid." To repeat, a great poet is concerned with fundamentals:

For thus his work will be sifted of what is transient and crumbling, the chaff of time and the stuff that requires footnotes. Permanent things, or things forever renewed, like the grass and human passions, are the material for poetry; and whoever speaks across the gap of a thousand years will understand that he has to speak of permanent things, and rather clearly too, or who would hear him?

16 Tor House and Hawk Tower, 1948

Dear Judas called major tenets of Christianity into question; *Medea* pointed to the violence at the heart of the classical tradition; "Poetry, Góngorism, and a Thousand Years" offered a pointed critique of modern art. If, in the Western tradition or in American culture, any pillars of belief were left standing after these assaults, Jeffers struck them down with *The Double Axe and Other Poems*, published in July 1948. His attack was so ferocious and so far-reaching that Random House famously (or notoriously) issued a disclaimer with the book, stating in a "Publishers' Note," that "Random House feels compelled to go on record with its disagreement over some of the political views pronounced by the poet in this volume."

The first section of the title poem, *The Love and the Hate*, was written before World War II ended, at a time when Jeffers' son Garth was still in harm's way, and when parents and wives were receiving telegrams from the government telling them that their sons or husbands had died. Such telegrams were falling "like snow / Over the country, silent and soft as snow, / Freezing the hearts they light on." Jeffers lived in dread of the day he and Una would receive one. When the war ended and Garth, like millions of other soldiers, returned home, Jeffers breathed easier, but he did not forget the soldiers left behind. Their anger, despair, and painful deaths were foremost in his mind.

The Love and the Hate combines thematic elements found in *Resurrection* and *Such Counsels You Gave to Me*. The story concerns Hoult Gore, a young soldier killed in the Pacific Islands campaign on or about July 9, 1944. After lying in his makeshift grave for three weeks, he forces his angry spirit back into his decaying body and breaks free, intent on returning to his parents' ranch in the Big Sur. When he arrives home, he confronts his mother, Reine Gore, who is in the midst of an affair with a much younger man, and baits his father, Bolivar "Bull" Gore, who is a member of the American Legion and a war-mongering patriot. "Did you / And your old buddies decide what the war's about?" he asks his father when he first sees him. "I came to ask. You were all for it you know; / And keeping safe away from it, so to speak, maybe you see / Reasons that we who only die in it can't."

As the story unfolds and Hoult's rage intensifies, he supplies his own answer: "we were sold to death / By liars and fools." He also unleashes a blistering tirade against everyone, including "the decent and loyal people of America" who, on a given Sunday, are in church "praying God / To bless their enemies: that is burn 'em alive and blast 'em / To a bloody mash." If he had his way, he tells his father, he would hang everyone who pushed for war from high gibbets: "You'll be there, old man, right along with the President" and all the other "pimps of death." As a reverse image of the resurrected Christ, Hoult forces his mother, like Doubting Thomas, to stick her hand in his wound. He also says, "This is my body / That was broken for nothing . . . this is my blood / That was spilled for no need."

But Hoult's return is fueled by fury, not love, and his goal is vengeance, not redemption. As he slowly destroys his mother (for whom he once expressed incestuous desire), eventually driving her to madness and suicide, he shoots a family dog, frightens away the hired help, murders his mother's lover, and shoots his father in the back. Of all these deaths, Bull Gore's is the most symbolic. When a rifle shot knocks him from his horse, he is paralyzed from the waist down—like President Roosevelt, America's leader. Using his hands to pull himself inch by inch along the ground, he is soon overtaken by the raging flames of a brush fire. "I wish that every man who approved this war, / In which we had no right, reason nor justice," Hoult says without pity, "Were crawling there in the fire's way with his back broken, and all the war-dead with all their women / Were here to watch."

The second part of the title poem is called *The Inhumanist.* The setting is still the Gore ranch, a few years after the events that transpired there. Reine, Bull, and Hoult are gone; their loves and hates have dissipated; dust covers everything they left behind. An old man, a caretaker who owns a double-bit axe, looks after the homestead. As he does so, people come and go, including trespassers, a murderer, his lost daughter, a gray-haired hiker, a German scientist, his own frightened doppelgänger, refugees from cities, robbers, a youth who wants to be a disciple, the ghost of Reine Gore, and fugitives from an atomic conflagration. A stray dog shows up as well.

The daughter, whose name is Sea-gull, is in the midst of an affair with a married man. She is trapped one day by the man's intensely jealous wife Dana Enfield, Dana's two brothers, and a ranch hand. After verbally lashing Sea-gull and striking her in the mouth, Dana orders her brothers to strip and whip her; they then add rape to the tortures they inflict. Sea-gull recovers quickly and soon runs off with her lover;

Dana, meanwhile, is murdered by her own daughter. Even though the caretaker does not know all of what happened to Sea-gull, he knows enough about the world to deplore "the evil, the cruelties, the unbalanced / Excess of pain" caused by humans. "I do not like the pyres of the martyrs," he declares. "I do not like barbed wire, squalor and terror. I do not like slave-sweat, I do not like torture." Repudiating Protagoras, Pico della Mirandola, and all others who place humans at the center or apex of creation, he says "Man is no measure of anything." In fact, as he considers the matter, he decides he would rather be "a stone at the bottom of the sea, or any bush on the mountain" than "this ghost-ridden blood-and-bone thing, civil war on two legs and the stars' contempt, this walking farce, / This ape, this—denatured ape, this—citizen." In one of his darker moments, he says "the whole human race ought to be scrapped and . . . ground like fish-meal for soil-food."

The old man's philosophy of life, as he conceives it in the course of the poem, is based on the presumption that "people-lovers" and "the human-centered" suffer from a narcissistic fixation that destroys the mind and soul. Consequently, he praises Copernicus and Darwin for pushing humans out of their "insane self-importance" and teaching them their true place in the world. Humans, the caretaker believes, are no more and no less than anything else that exists. They—we—are part of a material world that, in its totality, comprises the body of God. The Supreme Being, as the caretaker imagines him, is "not a tribal nor an anthropoid God. / Not a ridiculous projection of human fears, needs, dreams, justice and love-lust." He is, rather, "a lion that comes in the night" or "a hawk gliding among the stars— / If all the stars and the earth, and the living flesh of the night that flows between them, and whatever is beyond them, / Were that one bird." With insights drawn from physics and his own experience, the caretaker states his position:

> there is not an atom in all the universes
> But feels every other atom; gravitation, electromagnetism, light, heat,
> and the other
> Flamings, the nerves in the night's black flesh, flow them together; the
> stars, the winds and the people: one energy,
> One existence, one music, one organism, one life, one God: star-fire
> and rock-strength, the sea's cold flow
> And man's dark soul.

Convinced that humans are connected to everything else in a seamless web, "that all things have souls, / But only God's is immortal," he believes it is imperative for people to awaken from their selfish stupor and see the "transhuman intrinsic value" of the phenomenal world, "the endless inhuman beauty" of the universe. There is "deep peace and final joy," he says to himself, with geological and astronomical time in mind, in the knowledge that "the great world lives, whether man dies or not. The beauty of things is not harnessed to human / Eyes and the little active minds: it is absolute."

At the end of the poem, when the caretaker encounters a dying fugitive from a world-destroying war, the caretaker gives himself to "contemplation of men's fouled lives and miserable deaths." There are two remedies, he realizes: death itself, which provides relief from suffering, and his own philosophy. "There is no third," he concludes, repudiating all other faiths, creeds, and doctrines.

As characters in narrative poems, Hoult Gore and the caretaker speak for themselves, even as they express some of Jeffers' own opinions. In the third section of *The Double Axe*, which contains shorter poems, Jeffers addresses his audience directly, sharing his thoughts about World War II from its outbreak to its conclusion and aftermath. His condemnation of America's leaders and the war itself is predictably harsh, as is his portrait of humanity. In one poem, "Original Sin," he imagines a scene at the dawn of human history when a band of hunters capture a mammoth in a pit and slowly roast it to death—"They watched the long hairy trunk / Waver over the stifle trumpeting pain, / And they were happy." By locating the propensity for cruelty in human nature itself—not in leaders, governments, and institutions—Jeffers places the blame for World War II on everyone. Thinking of the day when the mammoth died, a beautiful day when the sun was shining and flowers stirred in the wind, he sees the excited hunters hour after hour roasting "their living meat slowly to death." "These are the people," Jeffers says, "This is the human dawn. As for me, I would rather / Be a worm in a wild apple than a son of man."

Most critics despised *The Double Axe*, condemning Jeffers for writing "a necrophiliac nightmare" and for adding "more than his quota of hatred and violence to the hatred and violence abroad in the world." As a "gospel of isolationism carried beyond geography, faith or hope," the book was denounced as "gruesome," "puerile," "truculent," and "a sorry exhibition for a responsible poet to have made." Most reviewers could not see or were not persuaded by Jeffers' complex aims, which he outlines in a preface:

The first part of *The Double Axe* was written during the war and finished a year before the war ended, and it bears the scars; but the poem is not primarily concerned with that grim folly. Its burden, as of some previous work of mine, is to present a certain philosophical attitude, which might be called Inhumanism, a shifting of emphasis and significance from man to not-man; the rejection of human solipsism and recognition of the transhuman magnificence. It seems time that our race began to think as an adult does, rather than like an egocentric baby or insane person. This manner of thought and feeling is neither misanthropic nor pessimist, though two or three people have said so and may again. It involves no falsehoods, and is a means of maintaining sanity in slippery times; it has objective truth and human value. It offers a reasonable detachment as rule of conduct, instead of love, hate and envy. It neutralizes fanaticism and wild hopes; but it provides magnificence for the religious instinct, and satisfies our need to admire greatness and rejoice in beauty.

The double axe itself—the implement in the caretaker's hand—serves as a concentrated symbol of Jeffers' overall intent. As both a tool and a weapon, with precursors going all the way back to the earliest days of human history, when *Homo habilis* came forth, the double axe provides a supreme, archetypal image of creativity and destructive power. "In Crete," the caretaker explains, the *labrys* was a sacred "symbol of generation." Long before the Greeks came, "it was a god, and they named the labyrinth for it." His own axe retains the marks of divinity, for in the course of the poem it laughs, screams, barks, yells, shakes blood from its eyes, stands guard, kills, swims, and climbs a cliff on its own.

Jeffers never reveals what the numinous object really is— perhaps he himself did not know—but it is clearly related to the sacred implement of Indo-European mythology, the thunderbolt (imagined as a hammer, axe, or two-pointed spear) of sky gods like Indra, Zeus, and Thor. One of the names for Zeus in ancient Greece was Zeus Keraunos (Zeus Thunderbolt); another was Zeus Labraundeos (Zeus Double Axe God). Both names refer to the lightning he generates: the life-giving, life-destroying energy that pulses from the divine heart of the universe. In Tibetan Buddhism, where the thunderbolt survives in the two-pointed implement called a *vajra* or *dorje*, multiple meanings are assigned to its component parts—some of which, on one end, are concerned with poisons (such as desire, anger, hatred, delusion, greed, pride, and envy), and others, on the other end, are concerned with antidotes (such as patience, compassion, loving-kindness, sympathetic joy, equanimity, inner strength, and pure awareness).

Ignorance and torment versus enlightenment and peace, *The Love and the Hate* versus *The Inhumanist*: these are the two points of the *vajra*, or the two blades of *The Double Axe*, which Jeffers hurled end over end at his readers, most of whom, as the critical reaction indicates, could not run fast enough to get out of the way.

The Double Axe was published when Robinson and Una were in Ireland, on what was supposed to be another long vacation. Prior to their departure, they spent several busy months with their sons at Tor House. Donnan, whose first marriage ended in divorce, had returned to Carmel from Ohio and remarried. He and his wife Lee had their first child, a son named Lindsay, in September 1947. Garth, who lived and worked in Europe after the war, returned with his German wife Charlotte. In December 1947, they had their first child, a daughter named Maeve. With two young couples, two infants, and two grandparents crowded into Tor House, life was a challenge and a joy.

17 Una and Robinson Jeffers, late 1940s

Robinson and Una left for the British Isles in June 1948. They planned to return home in September, after revisiting many of their favorite places in Ireland, Scotland, and England. One of their first stops was Donegal, on the northern coast of Ireland. From there, in July, they journeyed south to Kilkenny, where Jeffers was stricken with a severe case of pleurisy. His condition was so serious that he had to be taken by ambulance to Dublin, where specialists were on hand to treat him. He remained hospitalized for the rest of the trip, almost dying in late August when an air embolism entered his bloodstream. For most of this period Una stayed nearby, providing what care she could. At Robinson's urging, she left Dublin for a few days in order to see the opening of *Medea*, starring Eileen Herlie, in Edinburgh and to visit friends in London.

When Robinson and Una returned to Tor House in late September, Donnan, Lee, and Lindsay were there to greet them. Garth, Charlotte, and Maeve had moved to Oregon by this time, where Garth's career with the United States Forest Service had just begun.

As autumn progressed, Robinson slowly recovered his strength. At the same time, Una felt more and more tired. Eventually, in January 1949, an "obscure abdominal infection" accompanied by fever and an abnormal blood count, required surgery. Una's infection was successfully treated, but other symptoms soon appeared, including an acute and very painful case of what was thought to be sciatica. Neither Una nor Robinson knew it yet, but Una's cancer had returned, and she was dying.

1950–1955

    In the terrible years of the Yezhov terror, I spent seventeen months in the prison lines of Leningrad. Once, someone "recognized" me. Then a woman with bluish lips standing behind me, who, of course, had never heard me called by name before, woke up from the stupor to which everyone had succumbed and whispered in my ear (everyone spoke in whispers there):

    "Can you describe this?"

    And I answered: "Yes, I can."

    Then something like a smile passed over what had once been her face.

These lines come from *Requiem*, a poem by Anna Akhmatova. They refer to the period of Soviet history, 1935 to 1940, when Stalin unleashed a brutal attack against his supposed enemies within the Communist Party, government bureaus, the armed forces, and the general populace. Millions of people, including Akhmatova's husband and son, were imprisoned, executed, or sent to labor camps in the purge led by Nikolai Yezhov (Stalin's henchman before he himself was executed). *Requiem* is a record of the torment Akhmatova shared with others as they waited day after day for information about their loved ones. "Can you describe this?" a broken woman asks. "Yes, I can," Akhmatova answers, accepting one of the poet's heaviest burdens: the obligation in dark times to face and tell the truth.

    Jeffers said yes to the task, too—when, in the storm created by World War I, he found his voice as a poet and vowed never to dissemble. His commitment to truth opened the past to him, deepened his experience of the present, and turned his gaze toward the future. As a result, his poetry acquired prophetic amplitude, drawing insight from all three dimensions of time and drawing power from contact with the absolute.

Jeffers was aware of this aspect of his work. The caretaker in *The Inhumanist*, Jeffers' alter-ego, is at one point compared to "Heraclitus's Sibyl," who possesses "harsh wisdom, unperfumed, untuned, untaught" and a voice that "reaches over ten thousand years / Because of the God." In "Cassandra," another poem in *The Double Axe*, Jeffers makes a direct connection between himself and "the mad girl" of Greek mythology, the daughter of Priam and Hecuba who foresaw Troy's destruction. Condemned by Apollo to speak the truth and yet always to be disbelieved, Cassandra, as Jeffers pictures her, has "staring eyes and long white fingers / Hooked in the stones of the wall." With "storm-wrack hair" and "screeching mouth" she cries out to her people, but no one can hear. "Poor bitch, be wise," Jeffers tells her, be quiet: "No: you'll still mumble in a corner a crust of truth, to men / And gods disgusting.—You and I, Cassandra." In "The Blood-Guilt," a poem written about the same time as "Cassandra," Jeffers looks back over his own career. "Having foreseen these convulsions," he says of World War II, and "forecast the hemorrhagic / Fevers of civilization past prime striving to die," and "having through verse, image and fable / For more than twenty years tried to condition the mind to this bloody climate," he asks himself, "do you like it, / Justified prophet?" The answer is no; he would rather be dead than right.

Many of America's troubles, Jeffers believed, were rooted in a profound shift that occurred in the first half of the twentieth century, when America, once a David, grew to be a Goliath. Already in "Shine, Perishing Republic," written in the aftermath of World War I, Jeffers could see America settling "in the mould of its vulgarity" and "heavily thickening to empire." By World War II, as he observes in a companion poem, "Shine, Empire," the transformation was complete: "Now, thoroughly compromised, we aim at world rule, like Assyria, Rome, Britain, Germany, to inherit those hordes / Of guilt and doom." The consequences, as Jeffers looked further ahead, were clear: "we and our children / Must watch the net draw narrower, government take all powers" ("The Purse-Seine"); "In Europe we shall beware of starving dogs and political commissars, and of the police in America" ("I Shall Laugh Purely"); "we have dreamed of unifying the world; we are unifying it—against us. / Two wars, and they breed a third. Now guard the beaches, watch the north, trust not the dawns. Probe every cloud. / Build power. Fortress America may yet for a long time stand, between the east and the west, like Byzantium" ("So Many Blood-Lakes").

War, for Jeffers, did not solve anything—as World Wars I and II both proved. Immediate threats might be met and enemies vanquished, but, given human nature, more conflicts soon appear. For America, according to Jeffers, this meant facing a new opponent, a titan equal in strength and determination to itself. As he predicts in "Teheran"—written in response to the 1943 parley of Roosevelt, Churchill, and Stalin, when the three leaders discussed war strategies and plans for a post-war world—"The future is clear enough, / In the firelight of burning cities and pain-light of that long battle-line, / That monstrous ulcer reaching from the Arctic Ocean to the Black Sea, slowly rodent westward: there will be Russia / And America: two powers alone in the world; two bulls in one pasture." He makes the same point in "What Odd Expedients": "The next chapter of the world / Hangs between the foreheads of two strong bulls ranging one field. Hi, Red! Hi, Whitey!" Along with that stand-off, which did in fact become a long Cold War, Jeffers foresaw another source of trouble: "Faith returns, beautiful, terrible, ridiculous, / And men are willing to die and kill for their faith. / Soon come the wars of religion; centuries have passed / Since the air so trembled with intense faith and hatred" ("Thebaid").

Before the 1940s decade reached its end, the Iron Curtain divided Europe; Israel, having declared its independence as a state following the partitioning of Palestine, was at war with Egypt, Iraq, Lebanon, Saudi Arabia, Syria, and Transjordan; Mao Zedong completed a communist takeover of China, establishing the People's Republic there; and the Soviet Union and the United States were locked in a battle for economic and military supremacy. In America, a combination of pragmatism and fear led to the Truman Doctrine, which met the threat of Soviet expansion with a policy of containment; the creation of the Central Intelligence Agency, which took charge of covert operations worldwide; the Loyalty Program, which subjected federal employees to mandatory background checks; and the House Un-American Activities Committee investigations, which sought to uncover evidence of communism in the Hollywood film industry.

In 1950, as the new decade dawned, Senator Joseph Mc-Carthy claimed that communists had infiltrated the United States government; he then launched a crusade to find and expose them. At the same time, J. Edgar Hoover used the power of the Federal Bureau of Investigation, America's police agency, to conduct secret and ongoing investigations of political leaders, artists, intellectuals, dissidents, and social activists in order to identify individuals who leaned toward communism or, in some other way, posed a threat to the country. The work of McCarthy, Hoover, and others who shared their convictions acquired new urgency when, in June 1950, civil war erupted in Korea. Communist North Korea, armed by the Soviet Union and supported in the field by China, and capitalist South Korea, armed and supported by the United States and a coalition of United Nations forces, fought for control of the Korean peninsula. At first, American leaders thought the war would be easily won. By the end of the year, casualties were mounting and the outcome was uncertain.

As always, Jeffers followed national and international issues closely, but his primary concern at this time was Una. In January 1950, with local doctors unable to treat her worsening condition, she was sent to San Francisco for examination by specialists. Surgery was considered but then rejected because X-rays revealed cancer up and down her spine. Later, Jeffers told family and friends that he knew right then that

Una's condition was incurable, but, following a custom of the time, he kept the truth to himself. As he explains in a letter to her sisters, "Una never knew that her trouble was cancer, and I think never suspected it, except once near the end, but I laughed at her when she suggested it, and I think drove the thought out of her mind. And of course I didn't want to tell anyone, for fear the idea might somehow be reflected to her."

Whether Una knew she was terminally ill is unknown. Soon after the doctors examined her in San Francisco, though, she sent a telegram to Noël Sullivan, a close friend in Carmel: "I am awfully sick please help Robin all you can." Since friends of hers had already died of cancer and since the treatment she received involved radiation and hormone therapy, she must have understood the gravity of her condition. To spare Robinson, however, she did not speak of it, just as Robinson, hoping to spare Una, kept silent.

With each holding death a secret, they returned to Tor House, where Donnan and Lee helped Robinson provide care. Una took the downstairs guest room—"a sweet room," as Jeffers describes it in a letter, where she could see "the ocean and rock-islands covered with birds, gulls, pelicans and cormorants; and the sea-lions passing; and the land-birds, quail and the singing sparrows and linnets, in the bushes under the window." Flowers surrounded her, along with books and gifts from friends. Her grandson Lindsay helped keep her spirits high. Good days followed bad until late summer, when disease and painkillers rendered Una unconscious. Even at the end, lying in a hospital bed, her intense emotions and love of language remained intact. "She talked a good deal," Jeffers said, and held unintelligible "conversations with imaginary people, sometimes angry and sometimes laughing." On September 1, 1950, Una's rapid breathing ceased, and she died in her husband's arms.

In a fragment of a poem in which Jeffers records Una's thoughts concerning burial, written as if she is speaking just before she dies, Una states her preference for cremation. The thought of roaring up in flame, she says, is comforting— "besides, I am used to it, / I have flamed with love or fury so often in my life, / No wonder my body is tired, no wonder it is dying. / We had great joy of my body. Scatter the ashes."

A Mass in Una's honor, requested by Noël Sullivan, was offered at the Carmel Mission; beyond that, there was no public ceremony. Her ashes were mixed in the ground beneath a yew tree in the courtyard of Tor House, where the ashes of Robinson and Una's daughter were buried.

At the time, and despite the vituperation of some critics (the sniping of Yvor Winters twenty years before had set the tone), Jeffers was still one of the most famous and influential poets in America. Also, despite his desolation, he remained exceptionally active. Nearly a year before Una's death, he had begun work on another project for Judith Anderson—a translation and adaptation of Friedrich Schiller's *Mary Stuart*, shaped in such a way that Anderson could play both Queen Mary and her captor, Queen Elizabeth. Accordingly, for several months—around the time Una was hospitalized in San Francisco—Jeffers was immersed in the worlds of both Schiller and Mary Stuart. The one returned him to the *Sturm und Drang* era of German literature and to Weimar Classicism; the other took him to the very heart, the psychological center, of Elizabethan England. As he worked on the project, sometimes during vigils beside Una's bed, his thoughts no doubt turned at times to the passions of his youth, when he and Una studied Schiller's friend, Goethe, together, and to the days when they built Tor House, their Tudor home.

Though this project eventually fell by the wayside, other collaborative efforts involving Jeffers and Anderson proceeded. In September, just a few days after Una died, Anderson informed Jeffers of plans for a New York production of *The Tower Beyond Tragedy*. In October, as Jeffers worked on revisions to the play, he sent Karl Shapiro a sheaf of poems for publication in *Poetry*: "Fire," "The Beauty of Things," "Animals," "The World's Wonders," "Time of Disturbance," "The Old Stone-Mason," and "To Death." In November he wrote an essay about *The Tower Beyond Tragedy* for the *New York Times*.

The essay, published as "'Tower Beyond Tragedy': Poet and Playwright Tells How He Wrote Drama Based on Greek Stories," was printed in the newspaper on Anderson's opening night, November 26, 1950. One of the reasons he turned to ancient Greece for inspiration early in his career, Jeffers explains in the essay, was because of the way Greek dramatists represented "elemental human nature" in eternally valid ways, especially when extreme emotion or behavior was involved. The story of Clytemnestra's murder of Agamemnon and their son's revenge also gave him a chance, Jeffers says, to express his own newfound pantheistic mysticism. After killing his mother, Orestes turns away from his family's legacy of crime and madness, which is the legacy of humankind, and embraces "the cold glory of the universe." In doing so, he identifies the path that Jeffers himself would follow for the rest of his life.

A patriot may identify himself with his nation, or a saint with God; Orestes, in the poem, identifies himself with the whole divine nature of things; earth, man and stars, the mountain forest and the running streams; they are all one existence, one organism. He perceives this, and that himself is included in it, identical with it. This perception is his tower beyond the reach of tragedy; because, whatever may happen, the great organism will remain forever immortal and immortally beautiful. Orestes has "fallen in love outward," not with a human creature, nor a limited cause, but with the universal God.

Jeffers traveled by plane to New York soon after the play opened, but the production, a one-month run produced by the American National Theatre and Academy, disappointed him. At Anderson's behest, so many lines were cut—especially from the speeches of Cassandra—that, to Jeffers, the play seemed flat and lifeless. Some critics agreed with him, but others, like Brooks Atkinson of the *New York Times*, were impressed. Atkinson wrote two reviews. In the first, he calls the play "a masterpiece": "the Jeffers poem is written in lines of fire that make an ancient theme seem immediate and devastating" and "Miss Anderson's acting crowns a distinguished career with a great tragic performance. No one should expect anything finer in the theatre." In the second, he praises Anderson's acting for its "terrible, burning vitality—animal in force but royal in purpose" and Jeffers for being a "modern poet who represents modern thought and emotion . . . in clean and pulsing verse."

The poems Jeffers sent to Karl Shapiro were published in the January 1951 issue of *Poetry*. In November of that year, they were awarded the Eunice Tietjens Memorial Prize by the magazine. Also in November, Jeffers sent Shapiro a copy of the narrative that would serve as the title poem of his next book. *Hungerfield*, the only poem published in the May 1952 issue of *Poetry*, received the Union League Civic and Arts Foundation Prize later in the year.

Projects involving Jeffers but initiated by others kept him in the spotlight. Judith Anderson's recording of scenes from *Medea*, for instance, continued to sell. First released as a set of 78 rpm recordings in 1948, the album was reissued in 1949 in the newly invented LP (long-play) format. Advertised nationwide by Decca, the album featured an essay by Jeffers about Greek tragedy, Euripides, and his own work. The album augmented Anderson's 1951 performances of *Medea* in Berlin and elsewhere. Also in 1951, Eva Hesse translated and adapted *The Tower Beyond Tragedy* for broadcast as a radio play by the Bavarian Broadcasting Corporation and secured the rights to translate *Medea* into German. In the same year, Blanche Thebom, a star mezzo-soprano of the Metropolitan Opera, commissioned Ernst Krenek, a leading Austrian composer, to create a work for her based on Jeffers' *Medea*. Eugene Ormandy conducted the Philadelphia Orchestra in the world premiere of *Medea*, op. 129, on March 13, 1953. Thebom's highly praised performance was preceded on the program by Respighi's Suite for Small Orchestra, *The Birds*, and was followed, after the intermission, by Tchaikovsky's Symphony no. 6, *Pathétique*. The same program was repeated in New York's Carnegie Hall ten days later.

Jeffers' first thoughts concerning his next book tended toward a memorial for Una. He considered a hybrid text consisting of *Hungerfield* (originally titled "Told to a Dead Woman"), a group of short poems, selections from Una's travel diaries, and selections from *Of Una Jeffers*, a memoir by Edith Greenan previously published in a limited edition. This plan was abandoned in favor of two separate books, *Hungerfield and Other Poems* and *Visits to Ireland: Travel-Diaries of Una Jeffers*, both of which came out in 1954.

Visits to Ireland was published by Ward Ritchie late in the year. The limited-edition book includes a foreword by Jeffers, a few pages of afterthoughts, and a modest selection of Una's diary entries from the family trip of 1929. The main purpose of the book was to introduce readers to Una, to let them hear her voice, as when she describes a round tower in Antrim:

A beautiful sight, that gray inexplicable "spear," seen between gray trunks of leafless trees. Behind it the winter sky of late afternoon, rose pink and pale green below, gray above. Great flocks of black birds, rooks no doubt, swarmed like bees about the tower's head, then swirled to the bare branches of the trees. To the right a moon, golden rather than white, in its first quarter. . . . We drove back to Belfast contentedly through the falling darkness. . . . Sign on shop-window just across the street from the hotel: "Adam Turner / Undertaker and Posting Master / Shrouds of every description."

Jeffers also noticed "shrouds of every description" during the trip of 1929, for that is when he wrote the collection of poems titled *Descent to the Dead*. Death was never far from his mind in succeeding years, but it returned in full force with *Hungerfield*. Published in January 1954, *Hungerfield and Other Poems* contains the title poem, a verse drama, and fourteen lyric poems.

The title poem tells the story of Hawl Hungerfield, a veteran of World Wars I and II, who lives with his mother, brother, wife, and son on an isolated ranch in the Big Sur. Hungerfield's mother is dying of cancer. In the dark beside her bed one night, he remembers his own encounter with Death when, as a wounded soldier, he saw the god-like figure walking among his fallen comrades. He was "handsome and arrogant" and contemptuous of the souls that so meekly obeyed him. When Death stood before Hungerfield and "made a sign, / Such as one makes to a dog, trained but not liked, / 'Come here to me,'" Hungerfield rose up with such rage that Death backed away. Of course, Hungerfield knew, the encounter was a fever-dream, occasioned by his bullet wounds. Nevertheless, a part of him still believed the experience was real. So, sitting in the darkness, as tightly coiled as a stalking animal, he was ready to leap if Death should materialize. Sure enough, just as a clicking sound in his mother's throat ceased, Death was in the room—with a sneer on his face, just as before. Hungerfield sprang forward and grabbed hold, surprised that he could actually feel him, and wrestled—like Jacob with the angel—until Death cried out and slipped away. For fifteen minutes that night, no one died anywhere; in the morning, Hungerfield's mother was well. She was angry with her son, however, for driving Death away and for returning her to a life she did not want. Eventually, Death has his revenge—taking livestock, a horse, Hungerfield's wife and son, and then, through Hungerfield's rage, his brother, who dies from a blow to the head. Staggered by these tragedies, Hungerfield burns the house down, with himself in it. His mother escapes the flames and lives for two more years.

Jeffers tells the story as if he is talking to Una. The poem opens with recollections of their life together, and then he addresses her directly. "I never thought you would leave me, dear love," he writes a year after she died. "My torment is memory. / My grief to have seen the banner and beauty of your brave life / Dragged in the dust down the dim road to death. To have seen you defeated, / You who never despaired, passing through weakness / And pain— / to nothing." He knows she cannot hear him, and yet he speaks as if she can. No sooner has he described Hungerfield's mother lying in her deathbed than he interjects his own cry of pain. "This is my wound," he exclaims in sympathy. "This is what never time nor change nor whiskey will heal: / To have watched the bladed throat-muscles lifting the breast-bone, frail strands of exhausted flesh, laboring, laboring / Only for a little air. The poets who sing of life without remembering its agony / Are fools or liars."

At the conclusion of the poem, after Death has triumphed and the Hungerfields are gone, Jeffers addresses Una again.

> Here is the poem, dearest; you will never read it nor hear
> it. You were more beautiful
> Than a hawk flying; you were faithful and a lion heart like this rough
> hero Hungerfield. But the ashes have fallen
> And the flame has gone up; nothing human remains. You are earth and
> air; you are in the beauty of the ocean
> And the great streaming triumphs of sundown; you are alive and well
> in the tender young grass rejoicing
> When soft rain falls all night, and little rosy-fleeced clouds float on the
> dawn. —I shall be with you presently.

The verse drama that follows *Hungerfield* is titled *The Cretan Woman*. Based on Euripides' *Hippolytus*, it tells the story of Phaedra, the young wife of Theseus, who is used by the goddess Aphrodite to punish Theseus' adult son Hippolytus for failing to worship her. In Jeffers' version, which tightens the plot and reduces some of the original's supernaturalism, Aphrodite fills Phaedra with a fiery passion for Hippolytus, so much so that she begs him to make love to her. When he refuses, her love turns to anger, and she tells Theseus that his son forced himself upon her. Hippolytus denies the allegation, declaring that he does not care for women, but Theseus does not believe him, and in a fit of jealous rage slays him with a sword. Before hanging herself, Phaedra tells Theseus the truth: Hippolytus never touched her. By the end of the play, Theseus is shattered. His wife and son are dead, and he is left to contemplate the consequences of his own credulity and violence.

The Cretan Woman was composed when Jeffers was convalescing from his 1948 illness in Ireland. He forgot about it until he assembled *Hungerfield*, at which time he revised the play for publication. Once again, using ancient myth to frame his own ideas, Jeffers draws readers into the maelstrom of the human heart, where love and hate, like magnetism, are two poles of one force. And once again, without making a point of it, Jeffers uses an archetypal story to comment on current events. Theseus, a traditional Greek hero, personifies the spirit of war. "It was you I hated," Phaedra tells him— speaking across time to all military leaders, especially those in the twentieth century who had done so much harm— "an old gray manslayer; an old gray wolf, stinking of blood, destroyer / Of generations. For fifty years you have been killing the sons of men—*and now your own son.*"

When *The Cretan Woman* was published, "the bitter futile war" in Korea, as Jeffers calls it in a companion poem, had just ground down to its clenched stalemate. According to government reports, 54,000 American soldiers were dead and over 100,000 were wounded. In three short years, from 1950 to 1953, the war took approximately 2,500,000 Chinese, North Korean, and South Korean lives. And when it was over, nothing had changed. The two sides faced each other at the same border, guns loaded, ready to fire.

"We are not extremely sorry for the woes of men," Aphrodite admits at the end of the play, speaking for herself and other gods. At the same time, she issues a warning to humanity. People who forget their place in the larger scheme of things and who believe they can shape their own destiny, are fooling themselves:

In future days men will become so powerful
That they seem to control the heavens and the earth,
They seem to understand the stars and all science—
Let them beware. Something is lurking hidden.
There is always a knife in the flowers. There is always a lion just
    beyond the firelight.

Firelight is the subject of one of the poems that follows *The Cretan Woman*. Titled "Fire," the poem opens with descriptions of different kinds of fire: a fire in a fireplace after all the people have left a dark hall, burning alone with a "gentle roar and incessant rustle and the embers dropping"; a campfire in the Big Sur, "a small red point" in the darkness, seen from above by a doe; a turf-fire in Connemara warming an old couple in a small hut; a forest fire roaring like a hurricane through crashing trees. Another kind of fire, "More primitive, more powerful, more universal, power's peak," can be seen in "The fire of the sun and stars and the pale sheet-fire / Of a far-off nebula."

It is this kind of fire that most concerns Jeffers here—nuclear fire, the kind "our people are playing tricks" with and hope to use to "blast their enemies." In November 1952, the United States tested its first thermonuclear bomb. The resulting explosion was equal to 10,000,000 tons of dynamite (compared to the 12,000 and 20,000 tons of explosive force contained in the atomic bombs used against Japan). A second test, in February 1954—just after *Hungerfield* was published—created an explosion equal to 15,000,000 tons of dynamite. In between these two tests, the Soviet Union also detonated a thermonuclear device.

As both countries rushed to build nuclear weapons and to invent a broad range of missiles to deliver them, and as other countries hurried to join the arms race, government leaders began planning for a MAD world, one based not just on the threat but the reality of mutually assured destruction. "Fire answered fire," Jeffers observes, thinking of the persistence of conflict through history and the likelihood of even greater violence, "Blood cried for blood; crime and reprisal, the bomb and the knife, echo forever / To no atonement: / Until annihilation comes leaping like a black dog and licks the dish clean: that is atonement."

After dreaming of flight for 10,000 years, Jeffers says in "The World's Wonders," men have "made it the chief of the means of massacre." The same can be said for atomic energy. As soon as it was discovered, it was "put into service— / For what?—To kill." This sad fact leads Jeffers to reaffirm, several times in the lyric poems of *Hungerfield*, the value of Inhumanism—which, he makes clear, is not the same as misanthropy. In "The Beauty of Things" he refers to "The blood-shot beauty of human nature," and in "De Rerum Virtute" he says "I believe that man too is beautiful." Human beauty "is hard to see," however, and "wrapped up in false-hoods." Moreover, human beauty is transitory. There will come a time when America—like Greece, Rome, and every other civilization—"shall turn and bow down" to Death ("To Death"); there will come a time when humans are no more: "the people are a tide, / That swells and in time will ebb, and all / Their works dissolve" ("Carmel Point").

For this reason it is imperative, Jeffers reminds his readers, for individuals to turn toward the outer, larger world. "We must uncenter our minds from ourselves," he asserts, "We must unhumanize our views a little, and become confident / As the rock and ocean that we were made from." Such a turn, as he declares in "De Rerum Virtute," leads to an experience similar to that of the captive in Plato's Allegory of the Cave, who, in freedom, opens his eyes to Truth.

One light is left us: the beauty of things, not men;
The immense beauty of the world, not the human world.
Look—and without imagination, desire nor dream—directly
At the mountains and sea. Are they not beautiful?
These plunging promontories and flame-shaped peaks
Stopping the somber stupendous glory, the storm-fed ocean? Look at
    the Lobos Rocks off the shore,
With foam flying at their flanks, and the long sea-lions
Couching on them. Look at the gulls on the cliff-wind,
And the soaring hawk under the cloud-stream—
But in the sage-brush desert, all one sun-stricken
Color of dust, or in the reeking tropical rain-forest,
Or in the intolerant north and high thrones of ice—is the earth not
    beautiful?
Nor the great skies over the earth?

The beauty of things means virtue and value in them.
It is in the beholder's eye, not the world? Certainly.
It is the human mind's translation of the transhuman
Intrinsic glory.

Reviews of *Hungerfield and Other Poems* were generally positive. Along with high praise, Jeffers drew disparaging comments from some readers, but most agreed with Charles Poore of the *New York Times* that *Hungerfield* represented Jeffers "at his best." Horace Gregory, writing in the *New York Herald Tribune*, noted the "serenity of self-knowledge" that distinguishes the book. "In taking the road beyond middle age," Gregory says, with reference to the fact that Jeffers was now approaching seventy, "few American poets have stepped so far with a more deeply expressed humility and courage. With this book and those that may follow it, Jeffers' contribution to the poetry of our day is of mature inspiration and accomplishment. His position is secure and singular."

In March 1954, just two months after the publication of *Hungerfield*, *The Cretan Woman* was performed at the President Theatre in New York; in May, the play opened at the Arena Theatre in Washington, D.C.; and in July, The Players Theatre, an avant-garde off-Broadway company, presented the drama at the Provincetown Playhouse in Greenwich Village. The latter production, starring Jacqueline Brookes in the leading role, was so successful it continued for over ninety performances, closing September 26, 1954. Critics praised the "color, power and majesty" of Jeffers' verse, the "storm and fury," the "relentless grandeur."

1955–1962

"My life is growing narrow," Jeffers says in an unpublished poem written in 1952, "my dear and eternal love has died, through whose eyes / I used to look at the world."

"Whom should I write for, dear, but for you?" he asks, addressing Una in another unpublished poem written at the same time. "Two years have passed," he cries, "The wound is bleeding-new and will never heal." Jeffers takes some comfort in the fact that Una is part of "the great dream of the earth," as the earth is part of a galaxy, and the galaxy is part of the endless universe—"But for me here," he tells her, "the momentary loneliness / Is hard to bear."

Two years later his grief is undiminished. In "The Deer Lay Down Their Bones," written in 1954 when he was sixty-seven, Jeffers describes a remarkable place he once found hidden in the mountains: a clearing near a pool where wounded deer (shot by hunters, Jeffers imagines) came to die. In the midst of bush-oak and laurel, where a sweet wind blew upward from a deep gorge and where the deer had "water for the awful thirst / And peace to die in," bones and antlers littered the grass. "I wish my bones were with theirs," Jeffers says, thinking of the hurt he carried and the remaining years of his life without Una. The thought of suicide crosses his mind—"why should I wait ten years . . . / Before I crawl out on a ledge of rock and die snapping, like a wolf / Who has lost his mate?"—but he rejects the idea in favor of ongoing experience. "Who drinks the wine / Should take the dregs; even in the bitter lees and sediment / New discovery may lie." As the poem closes, Jeffers thinks once again of the hidden refuge he had found: "The deer in that beautiful place lay down their bones: I must wear mine."

He proceeded as long as he could just as he had before—with writing and thinking in the morning, stone work and chores in the afternoon, reading by the fire at night. "They have built streets around us," he laments in "The Last Conservative," referring to a bigger and busier Carmel, "new houses / Line them and cars obsess them," but, he adds, "The ocean at least is not changed at all, / Cold, grim and faithful," and the trees he planted still stand, "Haunted by long gray squirrels and hoarse herons," and Tor House remained a part of the natural world: "hark the quail, running on the low roof's worn shingles / Their little feet patter like rain-drops."

Jeffers published only three more poems in his lifetime, two of which—"Animula" and "The Shears"—appeared in an anthology of contemporary fiction, drama, poetry, and criticism drawn from around the world. The semi-annual anthology, titled *New World Writing* and published by New American Library in April 1954, featured a poem by Wallace Stevens, one by William Carlos Williams, two by Jeffers, and a dozen more by younger poets, all chosen by Richard Eberhart.

New World Writing sought to provide readers with "A New Adventure in Modern Reading." For the seventh edition, released in April 1955, editors selected an essay titled "Poet Without Critics" by Horace Gregory. The essay builds upon an issue first raised by Gregory in his review of Jeffers' *Hungerfield*. "A man from Mars, or less remotely, a visitor from Europe," he observed there, "might well ask those who talk of poets and poetry in the United States a pertinent question: 'Why does so much deep silence surround the name of Robinson Jeffers?'" With reference to professional literary critics and scholars, not to general readers and the theatergoing public, Gregory answers his own question in several ways. "In critical circles, right, left, or center," he asserts, with Jeffers' condemnation of America, his opposition to war, and other issues in mind, "his candid opinions, plainly said in verse, continue to be unpopular." Also, Gregory says, people tend not to speak of what they do not understand: Jeffers "is often misread merely as a prophet of doom and of mindless destruction." Finally, given the bias of most academic critics—whereby short poems characterized by ambiguity are more highly regarded than long poems that tell a coherent story—Jeffers is an anomaly. His "writings cannot be analyzed by the use of critical formulae," Gregory argues, "they are at once too directly spoken and, beneath their surfaces, too deeply felt and too complex."

Accordingly, as Gregory asserts in "Poet Without Critics," Jeffers deserves renewed attention. "At the moment there are good reasons for rereading the poetry of Robinson Jeffers," he says, describing him as "a singular figure in American letters" and "a 'poet' in the European sense of the word." Since Jeffers "is well removed from the kind of company where poetry is 'taught' so as to be understood, where critics and reviewers are known to be instructors of literature in colleges and universities," he can be approached freshly, with unprejudiced, open eyes.

Those who choose to reread Jeffers, Gregory argues, will find a body of work that contains flaws—such as repellent scenes of sexuality and a general lack of humor—along with a richness that ranks "among the major accomplishments in twentieth-century poetry." For richness, Gregory points to Jeffers' highly individual combination of California locale, biblical and Greco-Roman themes, Elizabethan detail, German philosophy, Calvinist concepts of retributive justice, pacifism, psychological insight, and technical skill. "From 'Roan Stallion' and 'Tamar' onward," he says of the latter,

Jeffers' technical contribution to twentieth-century poetry has been the mastery of alternate ten and five stress lines in narrative verse; in some of his shorter poems and in passages of some of his dramatic sequences, he employs a five and three stress variation of his narrative line. In this particular art no living poet has equaled him, and no other poet in America, from Philip Freneau to E. A. Robinson, has developed a narrative style of greater force, brilliance, and variety than his.

While acknowledging that Jeffers "has shocked people of rigidly fixed political opinions" and that his poems contain "prophecies which at the moment of publication seemed wrongheaded, probably mad, or wilfully truculent," the fact is, "time has proved Jeffers right more frequently than his adverse readers had thought possible," and "he has gone to war in the cause of peace." With his emotional fervor, honesty, and lack of personal vanity, Gregory concludes, "Jeffers has re-established the position of the poet as one of singular dignity and courage."

With each passing year after Una died, Jeffers withdrew further from public life, but he was not forgotten, as his presence in *New World Writing* attests. Early in 1955, Jeffers' *Hungerfield and Other Poems* received a special Borestone Mountain Poetry Award. *Hungerfield* was also nominated for a National Book Award that year. At the same time, the Columbia Pictures Corporation announced its acquisition of the screen rights to *Roan Stallion, Thurso's Landing, The Women at Point Sur,* and *Give Your Heart to the Hawks.* In June 1955, Occidental College commemorated the fiftieth anniversary of Jeffers' graduation with a special program (which Jeffers declined to attend) featuring an address by Lawrence Clark Powell. Also in June, Judith Anderson performed *Medea* in Paris as part of a "Salute to France" initiative sponsored by the American National Theatre and Academy. The six-week program, endorsed by the

18 Robinson Jeffers, 1956

governments of America and France but privately financed, was designed to further goodwill between the nations. Along with *Medea*, special productions of *Oklahoma!* by Rodgers and Hammerstein and *The Skin of Our Teeth* by Thornton Wilder were presented. The New York City Ballet, featuring Maria Tallchief and André Eglevsky, and the Philadelphia Orchestra under the direction of Eugene Ormandy also participated in the landmark cultural exchange. At the same time, a Paris publisher prepared a French edition of Jeffers' work—*Médée*, translated by Julien Philbert. Jeffers reached yet another audience later in the year when Anderson toured her native Australia with a production of *Medea*.

In February 1956, Jeffers left Tor House for a projected six-month visit to the British Isles with Donnan, Lee, and their children Lindsay and Una (born in December 1951). He and his family sailed from San Francisco, having booked passage on a ship that would take them through the Panama Canal. After arriving in Southampton, they meandered around England, drove up through Scotland, and then made their way to Ireland. In June, Jeffers abruptly left the British Isles and returned home, having received word that a Carmel committee had prepared a general plan that included provisions for turning Tor House and its surrounding grounds into a community park. To prevent this from happening and to protect the interests of Garth and Donnan, Jeffers decided to sell a few lots—thinking that if other houses were built nearby, there would be less public interest in his property.

The year 1956 was eventful in other ways as well. Random House published a special edition of *The Loving Shepherdess* designed by Merle Armitage and illustrated by Jean Kellogg; the Book Club of California prepared a keepsake edition of *Themes in My Poems*, a text based on Jeffers' 1941 lectures at the Library of Congress, Harvard University, and other institutions; Eric Bentley included *The Cretan Woman*, described as "surely one of the finest of American plays," in *From the Modern Repertoire*, his three-volume anthology of world drama; and the University of Michigan Press published *The Loyalties of Robinson Jeffers*, a study by Radcliffe Squires.

In some respects, Squires' book served as an answer to Gregory's call for a fresh critical appraisal of Jeffers, one undertaken in light of the apparent neglect and misunderstanding surrounding him. In chapters designed to meet the needs of an academic audience—with such titles as "Nietzsche and Schopenhauer," "The Anatomy of Violence," "The Inhumanist," and "Whitman, Lucretius, and Jeffers"—Squires sets Jeffers' ideas within the larger context of literary and philosophical history, intending thereby to help students and scholars "discover his world."

Reviews of the book were mostly appreciative, but some readers expressed ongoing uncertainty about Jeffers' place in America's literary canon. One reader, Kenneth Rexroth, used his review of Squires' book to denounce Jeffers. "In recent years," Rexroth asserts at the outset of an essay published in the August 10, 1957 issue of the *Saturday Review*, "the stock of Robinson Jeffers has fallen; for an entire literary generation it might be said to have plummeted and still be plummeting." Though he knew for a fact that at least one poet in his circle, William Everson, considered himself a disciple of Jeffers and others read him closely, Rexroth makes a sweeping claim: "Few young poets of my acquaintance, and I know most of them, have ever opened one of his books." Then, with an ironic smile and measured voice ("I say all this with distaste") that cannot conceal his fury, Rexroth launches an attack, dismissing Jeffers' life-work as "ridiculous," "shoddy," and "pretentious." "His reworkings of Greek tragic plots make me shudder at their vulgarity," Rexroth declares, and "his lyrics and reveries of the California landscape seem to me to suffer in almost every line from the most childish laboring of the pathetic fallacy." In bringing his essay to a close, Rexroth accuses Jeffers of "intellectual dishonesty" and describes Squires' effort as a failure: "You can't make an intellectual silk purse out of fustian and rodomontade."

When the *Monterey Peninsula Herald* reprinted Rexroth's essay on its August 14, 1957 editorial page, several readers complained. In response to an apology from the owner of the newspaper, Jeffers downplayed the incident. "I have suffered the same kind of thing more than once before," he said, "and remain mosquito-proof."

As he entered his final years, Jeffers was not the "good gray poet" that Whitman became, reaching out to embrace America and hoping America would embrace him; nor was he like Emily Dickinson, the "nun of Amherst," who lived and worked almost entirely alone. He was a blend of the two—a public solitary unmoved, at the core of his being, by favor or disdain. "A poet is one who listens / To nature and his own heart," Jeffers says in "Let Them Alone," affirming an artist's need for independence. "If the noise of the world grows up around him, and if he is tough enough, / He can shake off his enemies but not his friends."

In the late 1950s, "the noise of the world" was most certainly growing up around him. During Jeffers' lifetime, the population of America tripled, climbing from 63,000,000 in 1890 to 180,000,000 in 1960. Much of the increase resulted from the baby boom that followed World War II, particularly in California, where the population swelled from 7,000,000 to 16,000,000 between 1940 and 1960. The onrush of people created a soaring demand for housing while the G.I. Bill and other programs put a home within reach of almost everyone. Developers rapidly converted farms and woodlands into suburban housing tracts, using mass-production techniques to erect block after block of nearly identical homes, each filled with a growing family and an avalanche of consumer goods—radios, phonographs, televisions, hair dryers, dishwashers, power tools, barbeque grills, filter-tipped cigarettes, soaps, deodorants, packaged foods, Davy Crockett hats, hula hoops, Barbie dolls, and anything else entrepreneurs could dream up, advertise, and sell.

To accommodate all the automobiles already on the roads and the 58,000,000 new vehicles manufactured between 1950 and 1960, the Interstate Highway Act of 1956 was implemented, which provided for a 41,000-mile freeway system to move traffic swiftly through cities, states, and across the land. With more and better roads came shopping centers, malls, and fast-food restaurants—like the McDonald's chain. The standardized products offered by McDonald's reflected America's concern with conformity at the time, as seen in such codified gender roles as the "perfect housewife" and the "organization man." Other noteworthy features of the 1950s included iconic public figures like Elvis Presley, Marilyn Monroe, and James Dean; rock 'n' roll; credit cards; *Sputnik* and the space race; Christian revivalism; Beatniks; juvenile delinquency; and a growing concern with civil rights. President Eisenhower, a military hero, worked behind the scenes to advance America's aims—covertly toppling the governments of Iran and Guatemala and picking up the tab for France's military efforts in Vietnam. At the leading edge of art and architecture, Abstract Expressionism (color field and action painting) and the International Style (rectangular grids of concrete, glass, and steel) held sway; both avoided any reference to nature, history, or culture.

Jeffers continued to write about all three. The last original poem he saw published, "The Ocean's Tribute," was printed by the Book Club of California in 1958. The poem begins with a simple observation: "Yesterday's sundown was very beautiful." Then, thinking of contemporary arguments against such declarations and modern culture's characteristic self-centeredness, Jeffers says, as an aside, "I know it is out of fashion to say so" and "I think we are fools / To turn from the superhuman beauty of the world and dredge our own minds." Returning to his main concern, the sunset, he describes a stately effusion of color filling the sky—"smoked amber and tender green, pink and purple and vermilion, great ranks / Of purple cloud, and the pink rose-petals over all and through all." The ocean, meanwhile, "refused the glory" and remained slate gray. Suddenly, a bright fountain shot up from the surface of the sea, then several more. "There were ten or twelve whales quite near the deep shore, playing together, nuzzling each other, / Plunging and rising"— "lifting," Jeffers says, closing the poem on a note of pure perception, as the spouts ignited before him, "luminous pink pillars from the flat ocean to the flaming sky."

In another poem written around the same time, "After Lake Leman," Jeffers records a similar experience, one that occurred during his childhood in Switzerland. Standing beside Lake Leman (Lake Geneva) one day, he saw a flock of wild swans rise up together. The rush of wings created a reflection—a "great white streak" on the shimmering "dawn-blue water." He followed the swans and observed their visual echo as they flew toward the Dent du Midi, a nearby snow-capped mountain. Then, for a moment, he saw a connection between them. The mountain was "white with snow like the swans." Its contour looked like "beating wings high in heaven." "It was there," Jeffers declares, reflecting on the experience as an old man, "and from the roses with rain in them / When I was allowed out of school one April dawn I learned how beautiful things are."

The "there" in this line refers both to an actual time and place in Switzerland and to a mindset, a visionary mode of seeing that Jeffers found as a child, rediscovered when building Tor House as a young adult, and returned to throughout his life as a poet. Drops of rain, rose blossoms, wild swans soaring, reflections of beating wings on water, snow-covered mountains rising to the clouds, whales breaching the waves, brilliant sunsets—these are all transient moments of being, fleeting events in space and time, unique in their particularity, yet belonging to one vast vibrating field of energy.

"The Ocean's Tribute" was printed as a keepsake by the Grabhorn Press in honor of an award bestowed on Jeffers. In October 1958, the Academy of American Poets gave him a $5,000 fellowship for "distinguished poetic achievement." Since the average wage in America was $3,674 in 1958, the award carried considerable value and prestige.

The late 1950s also brought increased international acclaim. An acting troupe from Tel Aviv led by Israel's greatest actress, Hanna Rovina, brought a noteworthy production of *Medea* to Paris; Kamil Bednář introduced Jeffers to readers in Czechoslovakia with his translation of *Mara*; and performances of *The Tower Beyond Tragedy*, *Medea*, and *The Cretan Woman*, based on German translations by Eva Hesse, were seen by audiences in Germany, Switzerland, and Austria. At the annual theater and music festival at Bad Hersfeld, for instance, *Medea* was a featured event. The production, directed by Ulrich Erfurth and starring Hilde Krahl, was presented outdoors in the ruins of a Romanesque church. In Vienna, *The Tower Beyond Tragedy* was presented at the Burg Theater, home to one of the most venerable acting companies in Europe.

Robinson Jeffers: A Study in Inhumanism by Mercedes Monjian was published by the University of Pittsburgh Press in 1958. In October 1959, Judith Anderson starred in a televised production of *Medea* that had an estimated audience of 2,300,000 viewers. Other productions, publications, and awards followed, including Czech translations by Bednář of *Roan Stallion*, *Hungerfield*, and *Medea* in 1960; editions of Eva Hesse's translations, published individually in 1960 as *Die Quelle*, *Medea*, and *Die Frau aus Kreta* and collectively as Jeffers' *Dramen*; and the 1960 Shelley Memorial Award, a $1,250 prize given to Jeffers by the Poetry Society of America in honor of his achievements as an artist. The Shelley Award was bestowed in January 1961. Also in 1961, Bednář published a translation of *The Loving Shepherdess*, and James Hart included a previously written essay by Jeffers in *My First Publication*, a book Hart edited for the Book Club of California. In the following year, Ezra Pound's daughter, Mary de Rachewiltz, translated *Hungerfield* into Italian, and Frederic Ives Carpenter published *Robinson Jeffers*, a volume in Twayne's United States Authors Series.

In October 1961, the *Sierra Club Bulletin* included a selection of photographs by Philip Hyde along with excerpts from poems by Jeffers in a feature titled "The Big Sur Country." Though the *Bulletin* had included similar spreads before, this particular combination of words and images proved to be especially fortuitous, for it served as the prototype for *Not Man Apart: Lines from Robinson Jeffers / Photographs of the Big Sur Coast*, a popular "exhibit format" book edited by David Brower and published by the Sierra Club four years later. The title of the book was drawn from the concluding lines of "The Answer," where Jeffers says "Love that,"—referring to Earth and the universe as a whole—"not man / Apart from that." This was exactly the message Brower, as president of the Sierra Club, and his associates wanted people to hear.

In a moving foreword to the book, Loren Eiseley compares Jeffers to Henry David Thoreau and other writers who, through the enduring impact of their work, speak for the wilderness—literally, in Jeffers' case. "Something utterly wild had crept into his mind and marked his features," Eiseley writes. "The sea-beaten coast, the fierce freedom of its hunting hawks, possessed and spoke through him. It was one of the most uncanny and complete relationships between a man and his natural background that I know in literature." Describing Jeffers as "a person of great emotional depth" who "suffered as only a seer can suffer in an age of vulgarity and material affluence," he extols the love that animates even the most agonized products of Jeffers' vision.

Eiseley's observations are reiterated by David Brower and Margaret Wentworth Owings in introductory essays that plead for heightened environmental awareness. At a time when the Big Sur was vulnerable to large-scale housing and resort development and plans were underway to mine Pico Blanco for its limestone, Brower and Owings hoped Jeffers' poetry, combined with photographs of the Big Sur, would turn people toward preservation. The photographs were supplied by Ansel Adams (described by Brower as "a walking concordance to Jeffers"), Morley Baer, Wynn Bullock, Philip Hyde, Eliot Porter, Cole Weston, Edward Weston, and others—all of whom shared Jeffers' passionate commitment to the wild California coast.

Jeffers did not live long enough to see *Not Man Apart*. Nor did he see *The Beginning and the End and Other Poems: The Last Works of Robinson Jeffers* published by Random House in 1963. This final collection of scraps and drafts, augmented and revised in the third and fourth volumes of Jeffers' *Collected Poetry*, is noteworthy for the intimate conversational tone established throughout. In verses that are sometimes titled, sometimes not, Jeffers creates the widest possible compass for his thoughts, as he contemplates his own life and death along with the origin and end of humanity, planet Earth, and the cosmos as a whole.

At home in a scientific paradigm shaped by astronomers and physicists from Copernicus and Galileo to Einstein and Hubble, and aware of new discoveries through association with his brother Hamilton (a leading authority on dual star systems), Jeffers thought of the universe in dynamic terms. From one perspective, he knew, the universe appears to be eternal: "It flows out of mystery into mystery: there is no beginning / How could there be?—and no end—how could there be? / The stars shine in the sky like the spray of a wave / Rushing to meet no shore, and the great music / Blares on forever." From another perspective, the universe seems finite: "The heroic stars spending themselves, / Coining their very flesh into bullets for the lost battle, / They must burn out at length like used candles; / And Mother Night will weep in her triumph, taking home her heroes" ("The Epic Stars"). A combination of elements from both theories seemed most likely to Jeffers. In "The Great Explosion," he affirms the notion of an oscillating universe:

The universe expands and contracts like a great heart.

It is expanding, the farthest nebulae

Rush with the speed of light into empty space.

It will contract, the immense navies of stars and galaxies, dust-clouds
  and nebulae

Are recalled home, they crush against each other in one harbor, they
    stick in one lump
And then explode it, nothing can hold them down; there is no way to
    express that explosion; all that exists
Roars into flame, the tortured fragments rush away from each other
    into all the sky, new universes
Jewel the black breast of night; and far off the outer nebulae like
    charging spearmen again
Invade emptiness.

Given this model, any given cycle—like the intake and outflow of breath, or, more exactly, the systolic and diastolic beat of a heart—lasts a certain length of time. A universe, that is, comes and goes over a span of trillions of years. As one dissipates, another forms. It is impossible to say how many times this has already happened, or how many times it will happen again, or whether the beat is fast or slow, but Jeffers regarded the creation and destruction of the cosmos as a transient event in the ongoing life of God. "He is no God of love, no justicer of a little city like Dante's Florence, no anthropoid God / Making commandments," Jeffers says in "Explosion," rejecting all attempts to scale God down to human size, "this is the God who does not care and will never cease."

Just as the universe as a whole has a destiny, Jeffers states, everything in it lives for a moment and then dies. Our sun, formed by the compression of gas and dust around five billion years ago, is steadily burning itself up. In another five billion years, after a massive explosion, all its energy will be gone. Planet Earth—spinning on its axis, orbiting the sun, spiraling at the feathery tip of a pinwheel galaxy, sailing with a cluster of galaxies, each with billions of suns, through the cold and darkness of interstellar space—will also disappear someday. While it lives, it is connected to everything else that exists, as is Earth's progeny. The whole universe is composed of the same matter, if "matter" is the right word for the subatomic foam of particles and interrelated forces that characterize existence at its most basic level. As Jeffers explains in "Monument,"

Erase the lines: I pray you not to love classifications:
The thing is like a river, from source to sea-mouth
One flowing life. We that have the honor and hardship of being human
Are one flesh with the beasts, and the beasts with the plants
One streaming sap, and certainly the plants and algae and the earth
    they spring from,
Are one flesh with the stars. The classifications
Are mostly a kind of memoria technica, use it but don't be fooled.
It is all truly one life, red blood and tree-sap,
Animal, mineral, sidereal, one stream, one organism, one God.

On any given planet, such as our own, organic life begins according to purely natural processes. In one long untitled sequence, Jeffers imagines youthful Earth as a mare in heat eyeing her stallion the sun. "Her atmosphere" (marsh-gas, ammonia, sulphured hydrogen) "was the breath of her passion" and the sun's "fierce lightnings" provided germinal power. From diverse molecules, amino acids, and proteins, life was born. Over time, as life—"a virus / On the warm ocean"—spread, cells formed, and then bundles of cells, and then organisms that grew to become, according to Darwinian principles, plants, animals, and people. The process of evolution, underway for nearly four billion years on Earth, will continue for as long as the planet lives. At any given moment, certain creatures thrive. Dinosaurs, for instance, grew from "little efts in ditches" to enormous creatures with "leaping flanks / And tearing teeth" that flourished for more than 150,000,000 years.

"Whence came the race of man?" Jeffers asks, thinking both of the environmental conditions that produced humans and the characteristics that set them apart. "I will make a guess," he answers, imagining a change of climate that forced apes down from trees, where the struggle for survival amidst fierce predators "made life / A dream of death." As a result of those conditions, humans killed out of pure terror; walked upright, ever alert to danger; invented fire and flint weapons to protect themselves; and "invented the song called language / To celebrate their survival and record their deeds." Of the ancient songs that have come down to us, most, like those of Achilles or Beowulf, are cruel and bloody: "Epic, drama and history, / Jesus and Judas, Jenghiz, Julius Caesar, no great poem / Without the blood-splash." A wound was made in the brain during those early eons of human life, a wound that has never healed. It was there that humans "learned trembling religion and blood-sacrifice." It was there "they learned to butcher beasts and to slaughter men, / And hate the world"—and to think of themselves as different from and superior to all other beings.

Through "shock and agony" humans survived. "Cruel and bloody-handed and quick-witted," they roamed the world, adapted to new environments, and steadily grew in number. Even so, distribution was sparse. After Rome fell, Jeffers observes in "Passenger Pigeons," a man from Britain, traveling through Gaul, journeyed fourteen days through the countryside and never saw another person. By the beginning of the High Middle Ages, about 300,000,000 people inhabited the planet—a relatively modest figure—and Earth remained covered in wilderness.

Reproduction rates rose rapidly after that: one billion people in 1850 became two billion in 1927 and three billion in 1960. "Now we fill up the gaps," Jeffers declares, commenting on that fact: "In spite of wars, famines and pestilences we are quite suddenly / Three billion people." For some, there is comfort in such numbers; the more people, the stronger and more important humans seem to be. For Jeffers, the exponential increase in population was cause for alarm: "Have you noticed meanwhile the population explosion / Of man on earth, the torrents of new-born babies, the bursting schools? Astonishing. It saps man's dignity" ("Birth and Death").

Looking toward the future, Jeffers saw humanity's demise, possibly as the result of another war: "We know that this century / Is devoted to world-wars; we know that an armaments-race makes war. To heap up weapons—what weapons!— / On both sides of a fence makes war certain as sunrise" ("The Urchin"). It would be comforting to think otherwise, to believe that people can build weapons and never use them, but no: "Fear, envy, loyalty, pride of kind and the killer's passion" are in our blood. Such inherited traits, deeper than reason and "terribly in earnest," are the primary determinants of destiny.

Even though the impulse to build and store weapons makes war inevitable, Jeffers did not see another major war on the immediate horizon. "It is curious I cannot feel it yet," he remarks in "The Beautiful Captive." Nevertheless, with each passing year, as tests make more places on Earth uninhabitable and the inventory of nuclear weapons grows larger, the likelihood of war becomes increasingly dire. If all the bombs "Went off at once they'd probably infect the elements and blight the whole earth," Jeffers says, but knowledge of that fact does not lead to a change in behavior. "When a great nation is in danger of being conquered / It will use the whole arsenal." As a result, he advises, "be prepared to die." In a global nuclear holocaust, which, in truth, could occur at any time, "Those whom the blasts miss, the air and water will poison them. Those who survive, / Their children will be dying monsters." Even if humans manage to avert another major war, something else will result in their demise: "The troublesome race of man, Oh beautiful planet, is not immortal."

One scenario imagined by Jeffers in a late untitled poem involves a rise in sea level as a consequence of global warming:

The polar ice-caps are melting, the mountain glaciers
Drip into rivers; all feed the ocean;
Tides ebb and flow, but every year a little bit higher.

They will drown New York, they will drown London.
And this place, where I have planted trees and built a stone house,
Will be under sea. The poor trees will perish,
And little fish will flicker in and out of the windows.

In the larger scheme of things, this is no great matter. "I have pitied the beautiful earth / Ridden by such a master as the human race. Now, if we die like the dinosaurs, the beautiful / Planet will be happier" ("The Beautiful Captive"). Besides, as Jeffers adds in other verses, Earth "will flourish long after mankind is out"; "far greater witnesses / Will take our places"; "the enormous inhuman / Beauty of things goes on." In time, "there will be no camp-sites in the wild forest, no cottages / Along the sea-cliff; there will be solitude / In the obliterated cities. If some quaint bulks of concrete remain, / Flood-battered dams or exploded bomb shelters, / They will have ancient oaks growing in the cracks and long grass in the crevices" ("An Extinct Vertebrate").

Jeffers was confident about the future because "the earth is a resilient wonderful thing, / It dies and lives, it is capable of many resurrections" ("Metamorphosis"). "Look where they've lopped the redwoods / Out of the canyon," he says. "This was a hushed and holy place." Where once majestic trees stood for a thousand years, with "the clear stream at their feet" and "the pulse of the near ocean reverberant among their masts," and where, before them, their ancestors had stood for a million years, now "All is destroyed. For little finicking redwood planks / The great wood's dead." Only desolation remains: grim stumps, raw earth torn by tractors, and a muddy stream. But come back in just two or three years, Jeffers suggests, "and see the vines hiding the stumps, the flowering / Bushes and vines; and here is the holy grass again." After a million years—not very long in geological time—"My God the place is beautiful! green sun-trap between the mountains, / The flashing stream sings in the light." With the sight of the stumps still before him, Jeffers thinks of another ruined place nearby—an abandoned Mal Paso coal mine, where "The sweat of men laboring has poisoned the earth." Only thistles can grow there, but they are more than enough to begin the work of reclamation: "acres of purple thistles, eight feet tall, gorgeously glowing."

To see the beauty of nature, to feel the connection between one's self and the natural world, makes life worthwhile. For Jeffers, there was no other goal, no other reward.

As he considered his life from the vantage point of his own approaching death, Jeffers thought of his ancestors—beginning with a "totally undistinguished man" in Wales or medieval Scotland whose name, Godfrey, changed over time as a result of "the Anglo-French erosion" to "Geoffrey, Jeffry's son, Jeffries, Jeffers in Ireland" ("Patronymic"). "Godfrey" means "the peace of God," which probably eluded his ancestor in life, Jeffers surmises, but which he found in death.

Along with his distant ancestors, Jeffers thought about his parents: his mother, "a rather beautiful young woman," and his father, "a grim clergyman / Twenty-two years older than she," both of whom remained a part of him. He was their first child, and his mother suffered to bear him. The use of forceps injured his right eye: "it remained invalid and now has a cataract. / It can see gods and spirits in its cloud, / And the weird end of the world: the left one's for common daylight" ("Birthday (Autobiography)").

In addition to his ancestors, Jeffers thought about his descendants. "I'll not be here," he says in "Granddaughter," looking ahead to the time when his granddaughter Una will have reached womanhood. "I hope she will find her natural elements, / Laughter and violence; and in her quiet times / The beauty of things—the beauty of transhuman things, / Without which we are all lost."

He thought about his own career as a poet and the hardships others have faced—how Christopher Marlowe died in a tavern brawl, and Keats ("Wild with his work unfinished") died sobbing for air in Rome. Poe, Burns, Lucretius ("leaving his poem unfinished to go and kill himself"), Archilochus, and Virgil ("In despair of his life-work, begging his friends to destroy it, coughing his lungs out") all suffered as they reached the end of their lives. But this, Jeffers believed, is the poet's lot, especially in the modern era: "The poet," like an eagle or hawk, "cannot feed on this time of the world / Until he has torn it to pieces, and himself also."

Jeffers also thought about Una. "At night by candle-light / A huddle of bed-clothes on the bed is visibly a woman dying, that dearest / Woman who has been dead for ten years," he laments in 1960. "Well, I am dying," he reports two years later, dating "this twelve-year disease of mine" to the loss of his wife. "I have loved once, one woman, and now no more. / The glory and the pain are forever past." Thinking of the difference between himself and Una, Jeffers says "I have to consider and take thought / Before I can feel the beautiful secret / In places and stars and stones, to her it came freely" ("Salvage").

Together, they shaped an extraordinary life. "Against the outcrop boulders of a raised beach / We built our house when I and my love were young," he says, recalling their early years in "The Last Conservative." The sea had once crashed against those boulders; ages after the waves receded, natives built campfires among them.

> But the place was maiden, no previous
> Building, no neighbors, nothing but the elements,
> Rock, wind and sea; in moon-struck nights the mountain coyotes
> Howled in our dooryard; or doe and fawn
> Stared in the lamp-lit window. We raised two boys here; all that we saw
>   or heard was beautiful
> And hardly human.

In taking leave of life, it was to the non-human world that Jeffers turned—to the "endless ocean"; to "the cold stones my older brothers"; to the gulls, "Gray wings and white," giving their hearts, their "wing-borne hungers," to the pure exhilaration of flying in a storm. Resting on a hillside after a hike one day, Jeffers watched a vulture wheeling high overhead; in narrowing orbits, it slowly came down to inspect him. "My dear bird," he says, "we are wasting time here"—

these bones still work, "they are not for you." But how beautiful the vulture looked, Jeffers declares in "Vulture,"

> gliding down
> On those great sails; . . . veering away in the sea-light over the
>   precipice. I tell you solemnly
> That I was sorry to have disappointed him. To be eaten by that beak
>   and become part of him, to share those wings and those eyes—
> What a sublime end of one's body, what an enskyment; what a life
>   after death.

Such an end would be far preferable to a conventional
burial in a cemetery, necropolis, or columbarium. "Put me in
a beautiful place far off from men," Jeffers says, identifying
more with "the quick deer or that hunter in the night the
lonely puma" than with people. He did not want a funeral
or even an expression of sadness, for he knew he would live
on in a way that was right for him: "Let no one mourn for
me / When I step into the silent chariot / And my daemon
drives—not to heaven or hell, but the beauty of the universe." Even the sight of a freshly cut rose prompts feelings
of kinship and thoughts about the ever-turning wheel of life
and death: "So we: death comes and plucks us: we become
part of the living earth / And wind and water we so loved.
We are they" ("The Shears").

Death—"heart failure"—came quietly January 20, 1962.
A rare snowfall covered Tor House that day. Inside, the
sound of the surf could still be heard and fires were kept
burning. Jeffers, weakened by a series of small strokes, nearly

blind, and lying in the bed where Una endured her long decline, simply stopped breathing. He was cremated soon after, and his ashes were buried in the garden courtyard of his home—in the same place that held the ashes of his wife and daughter and, in time, would hold those of his sons.

A passage from *The Tower Beyond Tragedy* provides a fitting epitaph, for it goes to the heart of what Jeffers found in both life and death. "I have cut the meshes / and fly like a freed falcon," Orestes says to Electra, as he tries to explain how it feels to sever the bonds of human self-centeredness and to experience union with the larger world.

> I entered the life of the brown forest
> And the great life of the ancient peaks, the patience of stone, I felt the changes in the veins
> In the throat of the mountain, a grain in many centuries, we have our own time, not yours; and I was the stream
> Draining the mountain wood; and I the stag drinking; and I was the stars
> Boiling with light, wandering alone, each one the lord of his own summit; and I was the darkness
> Outside the stars, I included them, they were a part of me. I was mankind also, a moving lichen
> On the cheek of the round stone . . . they have not made words for it, to go behind things, beyond hours and ages,
> And be all things in all time, in their returns and passages, in the motionless and timeless centre,
> In the white of the fire . . . how can I express the excellence I have found, that has no color but clearness;

No honey but ecstasy; nothing wrought nor remembered; no
   undertone nor silver second murmur
That rings in love's voice, I and my loved are one; no desire but
   fulfilled; no passion but peace,
The pure flame and the white, fierier than any passion; no time but
   spheral eternity.

19 Big Sur, California, 1935

CONCLUSION

"Very like leaves / upon this earth are the generations of men," says one warrior to another in the passage from *The Iliad* that opens this biography. The lines are spoken by Glaukos, a Trojan, when Diomedes, a Greek, meets him on the battlefield and asks "Who are you?" Glaukos answers, "Why ask my birth, Diomedes?"—as if to say, "it makes no difference; like you, I am just a soldier here." Glaukos then speaks the lines above, in which human life is compared to the appearance and disappearance of leaves: "old leaves, cast on the ground by wind, young leaves / the greening forest bears when spring comes in. / So mortals pass; one generation flowers / even as another dies away." In Homer's luminous world there is always time to talk, even in the midst of battle, so Glaukos proceeds to tell Diomedes the story of his ancestors. As it turns out, their grandfathers once made a pact with each other, promising friendship between themselves and their descendants forever. Honoring this, the two warriors exchange armor, wish each other well, and part—each to meet his doom another day.

In truth, generations come and generations go, each with its soldiers, kings, merchants, and farmers, its men and women struggling to find their way in the world, its poets. Jeffers' generation lived through an exceptional moment in human history and passed away. Amy Lowell, Sara Teasdale, Edna St. Vincent Millay, and Wallace Stevens died before

Jeffers. Hilda Doolittle, E. E. Cummings, William Carlos Williams, Robert Frost, and T. S. Eliot died around the same time. Carl Sandburg, Marianne Moore, Ezra Pound, and Archibald MacLeish died later. All of these poets, together, extended the reach of poetry as they pursued, with freedom and daring, new forms of thought and new means of expression. "To break the pentameter," said Ezra Pound, referring to one of many innovations, "that was the first heave." As a result of their efforts, the field of poetry was completely open for the writers who came after them.

If asked directly, Jeffers' response to the question "Who are you?" would most likely be similar to Glaukos'. Shy and self-effacing by nature, he tended to brush such queries aside. Preferring to avoid the spotlight, he did not contribute very often to literary journals, say much about his own verse (or anyone else's), engage in literary battles, appear regularly at readings and book-signing events, or write an autobiography. The life of a celebrity was not for him. As he says in his essay on Góngorism, "to be pursued by idlers and autograph hunters and inquiring admirers, would surely be a sad nuisance. And it is destructive, too, if you take it seriously; it wastes your energy into self-consciousness; it destroys spontaneity and soils the springs of the mind." Later in the same essay, he offers an observation about poetry that could also be applied to himself and to his life's work:

I have no sympathy with the notion that the world owes a duty to poetry, or any other art. Poetry is not a civilizer, rather the reverse, for great poetry appeals to the most primitive instincts. It is not necessarily a moralizer; it does not necessarily improve one's character; it does not even teach good manners. It is a beautiful work of nature, like an eagle or a high sunrise. You owe it no duty. If you like it, listen to it; if not, let it alone.

Those who listen to Jeffers hear an uncommon voice.

No other modern poet had a childhood quite like his—where an understanding of European civilization was acquired *in situ*; where Greek, Latin, French, German, and English were learned and used simultaneously; and where a close study of the biblical tradition was considered routine. In adulthood, many of Jeffers' contemporaries turned toward Europe, some choosing to live there for the better part of their lives. Others turned their backs on the old world, preferring to set their artistic roots in American soil. Virtually all lived on either side of the Atlantic—on the eastern seaboard of America or in such countries as England, France, and Italy. A few lived as far west as Chicago. Jeffers alone, however, left the east coast with his parents and traveled across the continent to the Pacific, carrying, as he makes clear in such poems as "The Torch-Bearers' Race," the Greco-Roman and Judeo-Christian tradition with him, taking it as far as it could go. Accordingly, he was the one poet of his generation to feel, in his bones, both the geographical "end" of Western Civilization and the closing of the American frontier.

Not only was Jeffers the only major poet of his time to reside in California—the one state in America during the twentieth century upon which the nation and the world projected its dreams—but he lived in Carmel, one of the most vibrant centers of artistic and intellectual activity on the entire west coast. When Jeffers first arrived there, Carmel was a remote, Bohemian village with no paved streets. The homestead he and Una created for themselves—consisting of Tor House, Hawk Tower, a garden courtyard, a hillside covered with wild flowers, and a grove of trees—grew organically from the natural environment. In all his years, there was never a moment he could not hear the sound of waves breaking on the shore. Most of his poet contemporaries, on the other hand, lived in or near large metropolitan areas, amidst the hum of human commerce. Their daily experiences and their concerns as artists were primarily urban in character, which is one of the reasons Modernism in literature is so closely identified with city life.

Jeffers' contemporaries channeled most of their poetic energy into the lyric form. They preferred to write short poems (or, in a few cases, long poems in a lyric format) that favored irony, abstraction, obscurity, language play, and other forms of inventive self-expression. Such a predilection conformed to and helped articulate the feeling of fragmentation that befell Western Civilization in the twentieth century, all the more so when such techniques as collage came into play. With no overarching conceptual scheme to contain their thoughts, or with only the search for such a scheme to drive them, poets moved freely from poem to poem (even from image to image within a poem), sharing perceptions, offering insights, capturing reality in a piecemeal way. In devoting themselves almost exclusively to the lyric form, though, they abandoned the two other major modes of poetic expression—narrative and drama, once the poet's stock in trade. Not Jeffers. From the beginning to the end of his career, he wrote narrative poems (including epics), verse dramas, and lyrics equally. No other poet of his generation did the same.

The narrative instinct is surely as old as human consciousness. It may even predate the advent of speech, serving for eons as a mute need to make sense of existence. *Mythopoesis*, Greek for "myth-making," refers to the efflorescence of this instinct in language, where stories create order in what otherwise is a chaotic world. One aspect of myth-making might be called *geopoesis*—with reference to the means by which, in traditional cultures, the sacred history of tribal territories is made known. Naming a mountain (or any other landmark), disclosing the deep identity of an animal or bird, explaining why a wild rose has thorns—all contribute to the web that is woven, the web that binds people to their immediate surroundings, making them one with ancestral lands. Another aspect of myth-making is *theopoesis*, which involves telling the truth about living gods: their expectations and demands, their cleverness, brutality, and occasional love. Like the gossamer threads cast by human imagination upon the night sky, the ones that hold stars together in stable constellations, stories create coherence; at the mythic level they provide the only answers humans have to ultimate questions concerning life and death.

Poesis of this sort, of this prophetic magnitude, is atavistic—and Jeffers was the only poet of his generation to create it. Within the limits imposed by the lyric form, others wrote beautiful poems about nature, but no one else devoted himself or herself to bringing an entire landscape to life in verse; and no one else was so persuasive in doing so that he or she can be credited with helping to inspire the modern environmental movement. With a combination of scientific acumen and aboriginal love for the Monterey–Carmel–Big Sur coast of California, Jeffers uncovered the *terroir*, the spirit and inner life of the region—as revealed in its topography, its flora, fauna, and people. If native storytellers from earlier times, even millennia before, could listen to Jeffers speak of Point Lobos (where *Tamar* takes place) and all the other haunted landmarks in the area, if they could see a hawk through Jeffers' eyes or hear in his rhythms the pounding surf, they would sit before him spellbound and marvel again at the world they knew.

Within the limits imposed by the lyric form, others in Jeffers' generation wrote powerful poems employing or referring to archetypes and myths, but no one else examined—as Jeffers repeatedly did in his narratives and dramas—their mysterious operation in actual human lives. A passage in *Roan Stallion* is especially telling. After California rides to a hilltop on the back of her beloved stallion, she dismounts and lies in the grass, dreaming. Jeffers, observing her from outside and above, comments on the fire in her mind:

> The fire threw up figures
> And symbols meanwhile, racial myths formed and dissolved in it, the
>   phantom rulers of humanity
> That without being are yet more real than what they are born of, and
>   without shape, shape that which makes them:

The nerves and the flesh go by shadowlike, the limbs and the lives
    shadowlike, these shadows remain, these shadows
To whom temples, to whom churches, to whom labors and wars,
    visions and dreams are dedicate.

Jeffers demonstrated the undiminished power of these shadows in poem after poem: directly, in such works as *The Tower Beyond Tragedy* and *Dear Judas*, where the foundational stories of Agamemnon's return from the Trojan War and Jesus' crucifixion are retold; and indirectly, in such works as *Cawdor* and *The Women at Point Sur*, where Fera relives the fate of Phaedra and Rev. Barclay inverts the life of Moses. At the same time, Jeffers never stopped looking at the fire inside the human mind, or soul, itself—the molten core of consciousness that lights all thought and feeling. California's ardor is taken seriously, as is that of Tamar, Judas, Clare Walker, Onorio Vasquez, Helen Thurso, Lance Fraser, Bruce Ferguson, Hoult Gore, Medea, Hungerfield, and all the rest.

Like other poets before him (along with scientists such as Darwin and Freud), Jeffers was most interested in the interplay of two archetypal forces—Eros and Thanatos, the sexual instinct and the drive toward death—both of which figure prominently in his poems. No other poet of his time looked so closely at the impact "Love" has on people or considered so intently what happens when individuals, nations, and leaders, including American presidents, are gripped by "War." If, as some argue, violence (desire and destructiveness commingled) is the distinguishing feature of human life in the twentieth century—inner violence and violence directed toward animals, people, and the whole natural world—Jeffers alone gave it its due.

Again, within the limits they set for themselves, other poets addressed issues of ultimate concern—Is there a God? What happens when we die? How should we live?—and, in searching for answers, wrote poems of exquisite beauty. For the most part, however, their work in this area was static. Some great lyrics written in the vacuum created by the Death of God speak eloquently about the need for a whole new conception of reality (without ever finding one); others offer moving reaffirmations of traditional Christian faith; but most poems written in the modern era conform to a secular spirit, whereby the idea of God—any image of a Higher Power—is neither resolutely affirmed nor specifically denied.

Jeffers, on the other hand, broke new ground. With a skepticism worthy of Pascal, who had doubts about the efficacy of both reason and faith, Jeffers questioned the entire intellectual and spiritual legacy of Western Civilization, ultimately rejecting two of its most important fruits: Humanism and Christianity. In the course of doing so, he did not abandon the past or succumb to the disenchantment characteristic of his age; rather, he turned Humanism inside out, claiming Inhumanism for his religion, and turned Christianity outside in, finding the suffering of God at the center of everything. The fact that Jeffers' holistic vision of existence conforms to prevailing scientific paradigms, offers a salutary code of conduct, and, at the same time, opens a new path to spiritual enlightenment, makes his achievement all the more remarkable.

In Jeffers' difference lies his distinction. Standard accounts of modern American poetry, that is, tend to identify two major camps. On one side are the poets who stand for tradition, Eliot and Pound chief among them. The literature of Greece, Rome, and all the world echoes in their work. On the other side are the poets who stand for innovation, poets like Stevens and Williams who are not so beholden to the recorded past, who seek fresh encounters with reality, and who prefer an American idiom. According to this division, H. D. belongs with the traditionalists, Moore with the innovators, and so on down the line.

Jeffers cannot be assigned to either side. With one foot in the old world and the other in the new, he serves as a bridge between them. This very fact makes it possible to miss him, and helps to explain some of the silence surrounding his work. An implicit argument of this book, however, is that Jeffers is essential to understanding ourselves, the twentieth century, and the world. No study of American history or literature is complete without him.

BIBLIOGRAPHY

Primary Sources (Poetry and Correspondence)
listed chronologically

Flagons and Apples. Los Angeles: Grafton Publishing Company, 1912; reprinted Aromas, Calif.: Cayucos Books, 1970.

Californians. New York: Macmillan, 1916; reprinted Aromas, Calif.: Cayucos Books, 1971.

Tamar and Other Poems. New York: Peter G. Boyle, 1924.

Roan Stallion, Tamar and Other Poems. New York: Boni & Liveright, 1925.

The Women at Point Sur. New York: Boni & Liveright, 1927; reprinted New York: Liveright, 1977.

Cawdor and Other Poems. New York: Horace Liveright, 1928.

Dear Judas and Other Poems. New York: Horace Liveright, 1929.

Descent to the Dead: Poems Written in Ireland and Great Britain. New York: Random House, 1931.

Thurso's Landing and Other Poems. New York: Liveright, Inc., 1932.

Give Your Heart to the Hawks and Other Poems. New York: Random House, 1933.

Roan Stallion, Tamar and Other Poems. New York: Modern Library, 1935.

Solstice and Other Poems. New York: Random House, 1935.

Such Counsels You Gave to Me and Other Poems. New York: Random House, 1937.

The Selected Poetry of Robinson Jeffers. New York: Random House, 1938.

Be Angry at the Sun and Other Poems. New York: Random House, 1941.

Medea, Freely Adapted from the Medea of Euripides. New York: Random House, 1946.

The Double Axe and Other Poems. New York: Random House, 1948; reprinted New York: Liveright, 1977.

Hungerfield and Other Poems. New York: Random House, 1954.

The Loving Shepherdess. New York: Random House, 1956.

The Beginning and the End and Other Poems. New York: Random House, 1963.

Not Man Apart: Lines from Robinson Jeffers / Photographs of the Big Sur Coast, edited by David Brower. San Francisco: Sierra Club, 1965.

The Selected Letters of Robinson Jeffers: 1897–1962, edited by Ann N. Ridgeway. Baltimore: Johns Hopkins Press, 1968.

The Alpine Christ and Other Poems, edited by William Everson. Aromas, Calif.: Cayucos Books, 1973.

Brides of the South Wind: Poems 1917–1922, edited by William Everson. Aromas, Calif.: Cayucos Books, 1974.

Rock and Hawk: A Selection of Shorter Poems by Robinson Jeffers, edited by Robert Hass. New York: Random House, 1987.

The Collected Poetry of Robinson Jeffers, Volume One: 1920–1928, edited by Tim Hunt. Stanford: Stanford University Press, 1988.

The Collected Poetry of Robinson Jeffers, Volume Two: 1928–1938, edited by Tim Hunt. Stanford: Stanford University Press, 1989.

The Collected Poetry of Robinson Jeffers, Volume Three: 1938–1962, edited by Tim Hunt. Stanford: Stanford University Press, 1991.

The Collected Poetry of Robinson Jeffers, Volume Four: Poetry 1903–1920, Prose, and Unpublished Writings, edited by Tim Hunt. Stanford: Stanford University Press, 2000.

The Collected Poetry of Robinson Jeffers, Volume Five: Textual Evidence and Commentary, edited by Tim Hunt. Stanford: Stanford University Press, 2001.

The Selected Poetry of Robinson Jeffers, edited by Tim Hunt. Stanford: Stanford University Press, 2001.

Stones of the Sur: Poetry by Robinson Jeffers, Photographs by Morley Baer, edited by James Karman. Stanford: Stanford University Press, 2001.

The Wild God of the World: An Anthology of Robinson Jeffers, selected by Albert Gelpi. Stanford: Stanford University Press, 2003.

The Collected Letters of Robinson Jeffers, with Selected Letters of Una Jeffers, Volume One: 1890–1930, edited by James Karman. Stanford: Stanford University Press, 2009.

The Collected Letters of Robinson Jeffers, with Selected Letters of Una Jeffers, Volume Two: 1931–1939, edited by James Karman. Stanford: Stanford University Press, 2011.

The Collected Letters of Robinson Jeffers, with Selected Letters of Una Jeffers, Volume Three: 1940–1962, edited by James Karman. Stanford: Stanford University Press, 2015.

Recommended Reading (Biography and Criticism)

Alberts, S. S. *A Bibliography of the Works of Robinson Jeffers*. New York: Random House, 1933; reprinted Rye, N.Y.: Cultural History Resource, 1966.

Bennett, Melba Berry. *The Stone Mason of Tor House: The Life and Work of Robinson Jeffers*. Los Angeles: Ward Ritchie Press, 1966; reprinted Carmel, Calif.: Tor House Foundation, 2007.

Brophy, Robert. *Robinson Jeffers: Myth, Ritual, and Symbol in His Narrative Poems*. Cleveland: Case Western Reserve University Press, 1973; reprinted Hamden, Conn.: Shoe String, 1976.

———, ed. *Robinson Jeffers: Dimensions of a Poet*. New York: Fordham University Press, 1995.

Carpenter, Frederic I. *Robinson Jeffers*. New York: Twayne, 1962.

Everson, William. *The Excesses of God: Robinson Jeffers as a Religious Figure*. Stanford: Stanford University Press, 1988.

Fleming, Deborah. *Towers of Myth and Stone: Yeats's Influence on Robinson Jeffers*. Columbia: University of South Carolina Press, 2015.

Hart, George. *Inventing the Language to Tell It: Robinson Jeffers and the Biology of Consciousness*. New York: Fordham University Press, 2013.

Kafka, Robert, ed. *Where Shall I Take You To: The Love Letters of Una and Robinson Jeffers*. Covelo, Calif.: Yolla Bolly Press, 1987.

Karman, James. *Robinson Jeffers: Poet of California*. San Francisco: Chronicle Books, 1987; reprinted Brownsville, Ore.: Story Line Press, 1995.

———, ed. *Critical Essays on Robinson Jeffers*. Boston: G. K. Hall, 1990.

————, ed. *Of Una Jeffers: A Memoir by Edith Greenan*. Ashland, Ore.: Story Line Press, 1995.

Monjian, Mercedes Cunningham. *Robinson Jeffers: A Study in Inhumanism*. Pittsburgh: University of Pittsburgh Press, 1958.

Nolte, William H. *Rock and Hawk: Robinson Jeffers and the Romantic Agony*. Athens: University of Georgia Press, 1978.

Powell, Lawrence Clark. *Robinson Jeffers: The Man and His Work*. Los Angeles: Primavera Press, 1932; reprinted Pasadena: San Pasqual Press, 1940; reprinted New York: Haskell House, 1970.

Squires, Radcliffe. *The Loyalties of Robinson Jeffers*. Ann Arbor: University of Michigan Press, 1956.

Tangney, ShaunAnne, ed. *The Wild That Attracts Us: New Critical Essays on Robinson Jeffers*. Albuquerque: University of New Mexico Press, 2015.

Vardamis, Alex. *The Critical Reputation of Robinson Jeffers: A Bibliographical Study*. Hamden, Conn.: Archon Books, 1972.

Zaller, Robert. *The Cliffs of Solitude: A Reading of Robinson Jeffers*. Cambridge: Cambridge University Press, 1983; reprinted Cambridge: Cambridge University Press, 2009.

————. *Robinson Jeffers and the American Sublime*. Stanford: Stanford University Press, 2012.

————, ed. *Centennial Essays for Robinson Jeffers*. Newark: University of Delaware Press, 1991.

Useful Websites

Robinson Jeffers Association
    http://www.robinsonjeffersassociation.org
Robinson Jeffers Tor House Foundation
    http://www.torhouse.org

INDEX

44, 211; tourism, 66–68, 83; during World War II, 138

Carmel Mission, 31, 175

"Carmel Point" (Jeffers), 186

Carpenter, Frederic Ives, *Robinson Jeffers*, 200

"Cassandra" (Jeffers), 170

Cather, Willa, 87; *Not Under Forty*, 49–50

Cawdor (Jeffers), 74–75, 223

Cawdor and Other Poems (Jeffers), 71, 74

Cerf, Bennett, 92–93, 118, 119, 123

Christianity, 5, 21, 24–25, 71, 75, 99–100, 149–153, 224

Churchill, Winston, 171–172

Clapp, Timmie and Maud, 68, 125, 128

Clare, Saint, 76

"Cloud, The" (Jeffers), 46

"Coast-Road, The" (Jeffers), 105

Cold War, 172

Collected Letters of Robinson Jeffers, with Selected Letters of Una Jeffers, The (Karman), 7–8

Collected Poetry of Robinson Jeffers, The (Hunt), 7, 8, 201–202

Columbia Pictures Corporation, 192

"Contemplation of the Sword" (Jeffers), 121–122, 135

"Continent's End" (Jeffers), 37, 48–49

Cretan Woman, The (Jeffers), 182–184, 187, 194, 199

Cummings, E. E., 1, 142, 218

Dadaism, 38, 52

Darwin, Charles, 5, 20, 75, 162, 205, 223

"Day Is a Poem, The" (Jeffers), 129, 131, 135

Dear Judas (Jeffers), 75–76, 149–153, 159, 223

Dear Judas and Other Poems (Jeffers), 71, 75–78, 80

death, 164; of civilizations, 4, 38, 39, 98, 105, 133, 186; of humanity, 4, 78, 202, 206–208; Jeffers' thoughts about his own, 188, 212; and life cycle, 98, 100, 208, 212; personified, 180–182, 186

Decadent movement, 19

"Deer Lay Down Their Bones, The" (Jeffers), 188–189

de Rachewiltz, Mary, 200

"De Rerum Virtute" (Jeffers), 185, 186–187

Descent to the Dead (Jeffers), 90, 91, 94, 180

Dickinson, Emily, 1, 21, 23–25, 195

Dirac, Paul, 109–110

Hunt, Tim, *The Collected Poetry of Robinson Jeffers*, 7, 8, 201–202

"I claim my natural choices" (Jeffers), lines from, 211

"I have loved once. . . ." *See* "I claim my natural choices" (Jeffers)

"I have told you in another poem" (Jeffers), lines from, 212

influenza epidemic, 39

Inhumanism, 111–113, 162–164, 177, 185–187, 208–209, 210, 211, 213–214, 224; definition of, 165

Inhumanist, The (Jeffers), 161–164, 170

"In the Hill at Newgrange" (Jeffers), 91

"Invocation" (Jeffers), 41

"Iona: The Graves of the Kings" (Jeffers), 91

"I Shall Laugh Purely" (Jeffers), 6, 171

"It flows out of mystery" (Jeffers), 202

"It nearly cancels my fear of death" (Jeffers), lines from, 175

Japan, and World War II, 137–138, 144–145, 185

Jeffers, Annie (Tuttle), 10–11, 209–210

Jeffers, Charlotte, 167, 168

Jeffers, Donnan, 44, 89, 118, 122, 167, 168, 174, 193; photograph, 53; and World War II, 139

Jeffers, Garth, 44, 89, 118, 122, 167, 168; photograph, 53; and World War II, 139, 147, 159

Jeffers, Hamilton, 11, 13, 122, 202

Jeffers, Lee, 167, 168, 174, 193

Jeffers, Lindsay, 167, 168, 174, 193

Jeffers, Maeve (daughter), 30, 36, 175

Jeffers, Maeve (granddaughter), 167, 168

Jeffers, Robinson: affair with and marriage to Una, 16–18, 27, 29–30; appearance and personality, 6, 115–116, 124, 129, 133, 201, 218; artistic awakening, 46, 48, 54, 101; astronomy, interest in, 13, 61; awards and prizes, 178, 192, 199, 200; birth and death dates, 1; childhood, 9, 11, 198, 219; children of, 30, 44; daily routine, 61, 71, 189; death premonition, 122; education, 11, 13, 14, 15–16, 18, 30; foreign language skills, 11, 13, 15–16; grief, 30, 32, 36, 41, 181–182, 188, 210–211; illness, 168; marital discord, 125–129, 139; name, 11; neutrality, 113–115; photographs, 12, 28, 95, 130,

Republic"; "So Many Blood-Lakes"; "The Soul's Desert"; "Stephen Brown"; *Such Counsels You Gave to Me*; "Teheran"; "Thebaid"; *Themes in My Poems*; "Theory of Truth"; "Time of Disturbance"; "To Death"; *The Tower Beyond Tragedy*; "The Truce and the Peace"; "The unformed volcanic earth"; "The Urchin"; "Vulture"; "Well, I am dying"; "What Odd Expedients"; "Whom should I write for"; "The Wind-Struck Music"; "The World's Wonders"; "The Year of Mourning"

Jeffers, Una: affair with and marriage to Robinson, 16–18, 27, 29–30; appearance and personality, 124; birth and death dates, 16, 175; diaries, travel, 179; marital discord, 125–129, 139; marriage to and divorce from Teddie Kuster, 17, 27, 30; mastectomy, 139; photographs, 29, 53, 70, 117, 167; suicide attempt, 127–128; *Visits to Ireland*, 179–180; and

World War II, 139; terminal illness and death of, 168, 173–175, 181–182

Jeffers, Una (granddaughter), 193

Jeffers, William Hamilton, 9–11, 13–14, 36, 209–210

Jesus, 42–43, 58, 75–76, 100, 110, 111, 150, 152–153, 160

Johnson, Spud, 88

Joyce, James, 51

Jung, Carl, 64, 87

Kandinsky, Wassily, 35, 53

Kangaroo (Lawrence), 26, 27

Karman, James, *The Collected Letters of Robinson Jeffers, with Selected Letters of Una Jeffers*, 7–8

Kellogg, Jean, 194

Knudsen, William, 134

Korean War, 173, 183

Krahl, Hilde, 199

Krenek, Ernst, *Medea*, op. 129, 178–179

Kuster, Edith (Emmons), 30, 67

Kuster, Edward "Teddie," 17, 27, 30, 67. See also Golden Bough, Theatre of the

Kuster, Ruth, 67

Kuster, Una (Call). *See* Jeffers, Una

Lao-tze, 110